Unlocking the Fountains

Unlocking the Fountains

Inspiration & Challenge from Biblical Rivers & Springs

ANDREW D. MAYES

RESOURCE *Publications* • Eugene, Oregon

UNLOCKING THE FOUNTAINS
Inspiration & Challenge from Biblical Rivers & Springs

Copyright © 2025 Andrew D. Mayes. All rights reserved. Except for brief quotations in critical publications or reviews, no part of this book may be reproduced in any manner without prior written permission from the publisher. Write: Permissions, Wipf and Stock Publishers, 199 W. 8th Ave., Suite 3, Eugene, OR 97401.

Resource Publications
An Imprint of Wipf and Stock Publishers
199 W. 8th Ave., Suite 3
Eugene, OR 97401

www.wipfandstock.com

PAPERBACK ISBN: 979-8-3852-6222-9
HARDCOVER ISBN: 979-8-3852-6223-6
EBOOK ISBN: 979-8-3852-6224-3

COPYRIGHT PERMISSIONS
Unless otherwise acknowledged, Scripture quotations are from New Revised Standard Version Bible, Copyright © 1989, 1995 National Council of the Churches of Christ in the United States of America. Used by permission. All rights reserved worldwide.
Amplified Bible (AMPC) © 1954, 1958, 1962, 1964, 1965, 1987 The Lockman Foundation.
Authorized (King James) Version (AKJV/ AV) Cambridge University Press.
Contemporary English Version (CEV) © 1995 American Bible Society.
Evangelical Heritage Version (EHV) © 2019 Wartburg Project.
Holman Christian Standard Bible (HCSB) © 1999-2009 Holman Bible Publishers, Nashville.
Legacy Standard Bible (LSB) ©2021 The Lockman Foundation.
The Living Bible (TLB) © 1971 Tyndale House Foundation.
The Message (MSG) © 1993, 2002, 2018 Eugene H. Peterson.
The Passion Translation (TPT) © 2017, 2018, 2020 Passion & Fire Ministries, Inc.
Names of God Bible (NOG) © 2011 Baker Publishing Group.
New American Standard Bible (NASB) © 1960, 1971, 1977, 1995, 2020 The Lockman Foundation
New Catholic Bible (NCB) © 2019 Catholic Book Publishing Corp.
New Century Version (NCV) ©2005 Thomas Nelson.
New King James Version (NKJV) © 1982 Thomas Nelson.
New Matthew Bible (NMB) © 2016 Ruth Magnusson (Davis)
New Living Translation (NLT) © 1996, 2004, 2015 Tyndale House Foundation.
Revised Standard Version (RSV) © 1946, 1952, 1971 Division of Christian Education of the National Council of the Churches of Christ in the United States of America.
The Voice Bible (VOICE) © 2012 Ecclesia Bible Society.

IMAGES AND CREDITS

1 Euphrates

arabcenterdc.org/resource/mitigating-conflict-over-water-in-the-euphrates-tigris-basin/

2 Jacob Wrestling with the Angel, Gustave Doré (1855)

Wikipedia

3 Monastery of St George Choziba, with Elijah's Cave, above Brook Cherith

Hardscarf, Wikimedia Commons

4 Israeli, Palestinian, and Jordanian youth call for Jordan River rehabilitation

EcoPeace

5 Polluted Kidron stream flowing past Mar Saba monastery in the Judaean desert

Seetheholyland.net

6 Old Well at BeerSheva, 1900-1920

Library of Congress, Prints & Photographs Division, Eric and Edith Matson Photograph Collection [LC-DIG-matpc-01381]

7 Mary's Well 1910

Karimeh Abbud (1893-1940)

8 Spring at Ein Karem

Wikimedia commons

9 Pilgrim at Jacob's Well

Author

10 Steps uncovered at Pool of Siloam

Ritmeyer Archaeological Design www.ritmeyer.com

11 Flowing into the Desert, at Wadi Qelt

Author

Other Books by Andrew D. Mayes

spiritualityadviser.com

Celebrating the Christian Centuries (1999)

Spirituality of Struggle: Pathways to Growth (2002)

Spirituality in Ministerial Formation (2009)

Holy Land? Challenging Questions from the Biblical Landscape (2011)

Beyond the Edge: Spiritual Transitions for Adventurous Souls (2013)

Another Christ: Re-envisioning Ministry (2014)

Learning the Language of the Soul (2016)

Journey to the Centre of the Soul (2017)

Sensing the Divine (2019)

Gateways to the Divine: Transformative Pathways of Prayer from the Holy City of Jerusalem (2020)

Diving for Pearls: Exploring the Depths of Prayer with Isaac the Syrian (2021)

Voices from the Mountains: Forgotten Wisdom for a Hurting World from the Biblical Peaks (2021)

Climate of the Soul: Ecological Spirituality for Anxious Times (2022)

Reforesting the Soul: Meditating with Trees (2022)

Treasure in the Wilderness: Desert Spirituality for Uncertain Times (2023)

Roads of Hurt and Hope: Transformative Journeys in the Holy Land (2024)

Another Christ: Rediscovering Jesus, Francis, and Discipleship Today (2024)

Transfiguring Life: Unleashing the Power of Paradox (2025)

CONTENTS

Introduction 1

PART ONE: *Rivers of Struggle*

1 Euphrates and Tigris: Sharing Courageously 15

2 Jabbok: Struggling for Identity 33

3 Cherith: Living with Paradox 53

4 Jordan: Renewing Creation 73

5 Kidron: Making Life-Changing Decisions 89

PART TWO: *Springs of Hope*

6 Abraham's Well, Beersheva: Achieving Unexpected Reconciliation 103

7 Mary's Well, Nazareth: Encountering the Divine in the Everyday 117

8 Spring of the Vineyard, Ein Karem: Listening with the Heart 131

9 Jacob's Well, Samaria: Transforming Perception 147

10 Gihon Spring, Jerusalem: Discovering Vocation 163

Bibliography 179

Introduction

*I will open rivers on the bare heights, and fountains in the midst of the valleys;
I will make the wilderness a pool of water, and the dry land springs of water.*
(Isa 41:18)

THE AIM OF THIS book is to unleash the hidden secrets and forgotten messages of the rivers and springs that flow through the Bible, becoming alert to ecological realities and embracing spiritual challenges.

It is a poignant symbol: a spring sealed up. It begins with the harsh reality: the closing of a spring prohibits the quenching of humanity's thirst and denies essential refreshment. When, in the biblical account, Isaac comes to water his flocks at the wells dug by his father Abraham (Gen 26), he is heartbroken to find that the wells have been sealed up by enemies. And so he sets about clearing them. Indeed, in time of conflict "every spring of water they stopped up" (2 Kgs 3:19). The closing up of a well represents not only the deprivation of water but the loss of memories and meanings in the landscape. Even in our own times this reality persists: since 1967 many of the Palestinians' ancestral wells on the West Bank have been locked by the military.

But this physical reality can become a powerful metaphor. In the *Song of Songs* the lover laments: "A locked up garden is my sister, my bride; a locked up spring, a sealed fountain" (Song 4:12, NHEB). The beloved seems, for the moment, inaccessible, closed up, barriers held high. But she is soon imaged as "a garden fountain, a well of living water, flowing streams from Lebanon" (4:15). And so, the image of the opening of wells and springs releases in us new hope:

> For the Lord your God is bringing you into a good land, a land with flowing streams,
> with springs and underground waters welling up in valleys and hills (Deut 8:7)

> By making the hard, brown hills sparkle with streams of fresh water and causing valleys to come alive with springs. I will see that gentle pools wait on the desert floor for the weary traveler, and great fountains bubble up from dry ground; (Isa 41:18, Voice)

This book uncovers hidden or forgotten springs in the sense of revealing the meanings of the rivers and fountains of the Bible, while at the same time opening our eyes to urgent environmental issues facing them today.

In the Bible, springs bubble up in unexpected places and wells become the focus of a whole community, representing hope and trust in the future. Springs represent sources of life in an arid landscape, the gift of life itself, while the wells speak of humanity's deepest thirsts, both physical and spiritual.

Shaping the Landscape of Earth and Soul

Meanwhile, like veins and arteries in the human body, rivers course through the pages of the Scriptures from Genesis to Revelation: from the first rivers issuing from the Garden of Eden to water the earth to the River of the Water of Life flowing through the center of the heavenly city of new Jerusalem. The Bible begins and closes with rivers of water, bespeaking creation and new creation: "a stream would rise from the earth and water the whole face of the ground, then the Lord God formed man . . . a river flows out of Eden to water the garden" (Gen 2:6,7,10). In the Apocalypse "The Lamb will guide them to the springs of the water of life" (Rev 7:17). The vision concludes: "Then the angel showed me the river of the water of life, bright as crystal, flowing from the throne of God and of the Lamb through the middle of the street of the city. On either side of the river is the tree of life . . . producing its fruit each month; and the leaves of the tree are for the healing of the nations" (Rev 22:1,2).

Indeed, rivers are the life-blood of the biblical landscapes, and settings of dramatic events. Cascading into ravines or meandering ponderously across flood plains, the rivers of the Bible carry the memories and experiences of the unfolding story of salvation. Sometimes running fresh and clear, or clogged with detritus of the ages, they are at once forces of erosion in a sacred terrain and a formative power that deposits and builds up, sculpting and reshaping the landscape.

Introduction

The rivers run silently or noisily within the pages of the Bible and their turbulence or stillness become a mirror of the soul. They create frontiers and thresholds, beckoning pilgrims to journey beyond limits or barriers. Rivers often mark a starting point, a place of departure or a significant crossing place in the spiritual and physical adventure of the Scriptures. Indeed, rivers and springs are archetypes of the soul, primal, elemental symbols . . .

Hidden Streams: Symbol of the Inner Life

The mystery of prayer can well be represented by the image of a river. The river is at once a primordial and eschatological image of the divine life.[1] Like a hidden spring or underground river, prayer is often unseen, unrecognized, elusive but having powerful influences. Prayer as a secret river remains something that cannot be measured or quantified. It is something essentially mysterious, but rises to the surface and reveals its presence in a number of different expressions. As Roose-Evans puts it: "This secret life with God is like an underground river...we cannot see it, but we know it is there. Like water diviners we sense its presence within ourselves and also in others. We know it is there, even though others may doubt and challenge its reality. God is an underground river flowing to the sea...The underground river flows through each one of us."[2]

The river is an image which reflects diversity and flexibility. As rivers have different characteristics as they flow through the terrain, from incisive fast-flowing torrents to meandering ponderous currents, so prayer goes through various phases and embraces different intensities. The diversity of prayer encompasses turbulence and confusion as well as contemplative peace. As a river will course through different geologies (the great biblical river of the Jordan itself flowing along a fault line) so prayer will encounter both resistance and weakness. Meanwhile springs can represent for us sources of spiritual renewal, bubbling up even in the midst of deserts and harsh terrain: they speak to us of new beginnings, fresh birthings in the spiritual life.

To understand the Biblical story it is important to attend to these features of the land, for they are important threads in the tapestry of the scriptural narratives, the context and matrix and often the locus of the workings of the Divine. They become, literally and symbolically, sources of faith.

1. See Graebner, *Sacred Waters*; Tweedie, *Rivers and Lakes of Scripture*.
2. Roose-Evans, *Inner Stage*, 129.

Present Ecological Challenges

But it is impossible for us to revisit the rivers and springs of the Biblical story today without attending to their present physical state of degradation and diminishment. When travelling through the Holy Land the pilgrim is repeatedly faced with a juxtaposition of sacred sites and places of raw need today. In this book the present ecological challenges facing the rivers and springs will furnish us with a hermeneutical tool for approaching ancient biblical stories, confronting us with demanding questions that become an interpretative lens refocusing and redirecting our attention as we approach the texts. In this book as we revisit both great and forgotten rivers and springs of the Scriptures within the Holy Land and beyond, we wake up to the present environmental dangers they face. This provides us with a theme or issue with which to revisit the biblical accounts, helping us to discover there elements and questions that have not addressed us before.

Voices from the Riverbank and Spring

To assist our quest, we go in search of those who have lived on the riverbanks in past times and listen to their ancient and abiding wisdom, which speaks uncannily to us across the centuries. Beside the springs we will catch the echo of the voices of those who have long pondered their significance, spiritual writers who can hearten us today. This rediscovery of the rivers and springs will simultaneously expand our biblical understanding, awaken us to ecological challenges and reinvigorate our life of faith.

The theme of physicality of the landscape meeting spirituality has long attracted me since I lived and worked on the Holy Land as Director of Courses at St George's College Jerusalem. In earlier books, I have explored the spiritual life through the imagery of the visible landscape. In *Holy Land? Challenging Questions from the Biblical Landscape* I led the explorer across the terrain of the Holy Land, allowing the physicality of the land to throw at us vital questions and raise thorny issues in spirituality. In *Beyond the Edge: Spiritual Transitions for Adventurous Souls* we followed Jesus into liminal spaces across the Land, entering "no-go areas" and unpacking the theme of crossing boundaries, in order to experience at once a radical letting-go and a startling rediscovery of the spiritual life. In *Journey to the Centre of the Soul: a Handbook for Explorers* we left the surface terrain of the Holy Land and ventured underground, exploring the spiritual life through the

Introduction

extended metaphor of subterranean and cave spirituality. We ascended the heights in *Voices from the Mountains: Forgotten Wisdom for a Hurting World from the Biblical Peaks* while in *Treasure in the Wilderness* we discovered a desert spirituality relevant to our uncertain times. Now it is time to ford the rivers and drink deeply from the springs of the biblical narratives.

Like pilgrims on a journey we share the joy of the Israelites in their wilderness song:

> From there the Israelites traveled to Beer, which is the well where the Lord said to Moses, "Assemble the people, and I will give them water." There the Israelites sang this song:
> "Spring up, O well! Yes, sing its praises!
> Sing of this well, which princes dug,
> which great leaders hollowed out
>   with their scepters and staffs."
> Then the Israelites left the wilderness and proceeded on (Num 21:16–18)

CLOSING FOUNTAINS

There are several reasons in the biblical narratives why springs may be closed up. Sometimes wells were sealed because of possessiveness or spite:

> Now the Philistines had stopped up and filled with earth all the wells that his father's servants had dug in the days of his father Abraham. (Gen 26:15)

On occasion the motive was fear of enemies stealing the precious resource of water or the fear of them cutting off supplies to Jerusalem if siege was attempted:

> After these things and these acts of faithfulness, King Sennacherib of Assyria came and invaded Judah and encamped against the fortified cities, thinking to win them for himself. When Hezekiah saw that Sennacherib had come and intended to fight against Jerusalem, he planned with his officers and his warriors to stop the flow of the springs that were outside the city; and they helped him. A great many people were gathered, and they stopped all the springs and the wadi that flowed through the land, saying, "Why should the Assyrian kings come and find water in abundance?" (2 Chron 32:1–4)

Wells were sometimes covered over in an act of deliberate concealment. In the face of Absalom's threatened takeover of David's kingship, Jonathan and his friend found a great hiding place in a well, which was skillfully covered over:

> Jonathan and Ahimaaz were waiting at En-rogel; a servant-girl used to go and tell them, and they would go and tell King David; for they could not risk being seen entering the city. But a boy saw them, and told Absalom; so both of them went away quickly, and came to the house of a man at Bahurim, who had a well in his courtyard; and they went down into it. The man's wife took a covering, stretched it over the well's mouth, and spread out grain on it; and nothing was known of it. When Absalom's servants came to the woman at the house, they said, "Where are Ahimaaz and Jonathan?" The woman said to them, "They have crossed over the brook of water." And when they had searched and could not find them, they returned to Jerusalem.
>
> After they had gone, the men came up out of the well, and went and told King David. They said to David, "Go and cross the water quickly; for thus and so has Ahithophel counselled against you." So David and all the people who were with him set out and crossed the Jordan; by daybreak not one was left who had not crossed the Jordan. (2 Sam 17:17–22)

Sometimes the desecration of springs was part of a strategy of conquest or attack, as in the time of Elisha:

> You shall conquer every fortified city and every choice city; every good tree you shall fell, all springs of water you shall stop up, and every good piece of land you shall ruin with stones.' (2 Kgs 3:19)

In our own time, as we noted, wells in the Holy Land have been physically and forcibly sealed in a bitter struggle to control resources and land.[3]

Indeed, the sealing of wells can even be a metaphor for divine judgement:

> Although Israel may flourish among rushes,
>   the east wind shall come, a blast from the Lord,
>   rising from the wilderness;
> and his fountain shall dry up,
>   his spring shall be parched.
> It shall strip his treasury
>   of every precious thing. (Hos 13:15).

---

3. According to Al Jazeera, "Israeli Forces Have Destroyed all the Water Wells in Northern Gaza."

Introduction

The biblical texts can see in the spoiling of a spring or river an image of compromise and lack of integrity:

> Like a muddied spring or a polluted fountain
> are the righteous who give way before the wicked. (Prov 25:26)

Symbolically, we may say that the wells of the Bible have been lost to us by a kind of corporate amnesia. It has often been the case that Christians have attended more to spiritualized salvation themes in the Bible than to the physical creation. Ronald Simkins, for example, points out:

> Biblical scholars have been exclusively history-orientated in their interpretation of the Bible. Biblical scholars have too readily dismissed the natural world from being a significant factor in the development of Israel's religion and culture . . . They largely ignored the role that the natural world played in the Bible; instead they emphasized God's activity in and on behalf of human history.[4]

We have, it seems, covered over the wells and forgotten the significance of biblical rivers by our own myopia and amnesia. We have lost, too, perhaps, the ability to fully appreciate the power of the metaphors of spring and river.

OPENING FOUNTAINS

In the joyous story of Genesis 29, Jacob's opening of a closed well not only releases its hidden waters but also opens up the possibility of a loving relationship with Rachel—indeed, the unsealing of the well opens up a new future for many:

> Then Jacob went on his journey, and came to the land of the people of the east. As he looked, he saw a well in the field and three flocks of sheep lying there beside it; for out of that well the flocks were watered. The stone on the well's mouth was large, and when all the flocks were gathered there, the shepherds would roll the stone from the mouth of the well, and water the sheep, and put the stone back in its place on the mouth of the well . . .
> Rachel came with her father's sheep; for she kept them. Now when Jacob saw Rachel, Jacob went up and rolled the stone from the well's mouth, and watered the flock of his mother's brother Laban. Then Jacob kissed Rachel, and wept aloud . . . (Gen 29: 1–3, 9–10)

---

4. Simkins, *Creator and Creation*, 2, 8.

As the Psalmist celebrates:

> You broke open the earth and springs burst forth and streams filled the crevices; (Ps 74:15, *Voice*)
> For with You is the fountain of life; in your light we see light. (Ps 26:9)

David represents the cry of humanity:

> David said longingly, "O that someone would give me water to drink from the well of Bethlehem that is by the gate! (1 Chron 11:17)

UNCOVERING MYSTERY

Jesus promises: "there is nothing covered up that will not be revealed, and hidden that will not be known" (Luke 12:2 LSB). Of course, a key theme of the Bible is that of revealing. Indeed, the gospels begin with a closed heaven been torn open at Christ's baptism and end with the rending of the veil that concealed the Holy of Holies in the Temple. The prophet might say:

> Truly you are a God who is hidden. (Isa 45:15 NCB)

but God says

> I will give you treasures concealed in darkness
>   and riches hidden away in secret places,
> so that you may know that I am the Lord,
>   the God of Israel who calls you by your name.
> Let the earth open up
>   so that salvation may blossom forth. (Isa 45:3,8)

In the New Testament, the Pauline writer weaves together the theme of mystery and revelation in Christ. The Letter to the Colossians prays: "I want their hearts to be encouraged and united in love, so that they may have all the riches of assured understanding and have the knowledge of God's mystery, that is, Christ himself, in whom are hidden all the treasures of wisdom and knowledge." (Col 2:2–3) Colossians marvels at "the mystery that has been hidden throughout the ages and generations but has now been revealed to his saints" (1:26).

Mystery becomes a key word in Ephesians:

INTRODUCTION

- "he has made known to us the mystery of his will, according to his good pleasure that he set forth in Christ" (1:9)
- "the mystery was made known to me by revelation" (3:3)
- "perceive my understanding of the mystery of Christ" (3:4)
- "In former generations this mystery was not made known to humankind, as it has now been revealed to his holy apostles and prophets by the Spirit" (3:5)

Such an intriguing theme lies in the background of this book. It is time for us to unveil divine mysteries hidden in the waters and springs of the Bible!

Who Is This Book for?

The book is designed to be used by both individuals and groups. Questions at the end of each chapter are provided to stimulate personal reflection and group discussion. Three readerships are in mind.

First, it is for those longing for discovery and adventure in their spiritual lives. It is for those needing "something more" in their spiritual experience, with a desire to go deeper and further in their spiritual quest.

Second, it is for those drawn to the interplay between ecology and spirituality. It will inspire those who want to find ways to relate their life of faith and prayer to urgent environmental concerns. It will equip preachers and teachers.

Third, it is for seekers, for those wanting to discover for themselves the astonishing riches of classic spiritual writers. The book will open the user to a wide variety of spiritual resources that will inspire the spiritual journey.

In house-groups it can be used as a Lent/Eastertide course, with five weekly sessions in Lent and five after Easter. Indeed, it can be used at any time of year in an adult education program. It is recommended that both individuals and course participants keep a journal or note book, in which to note and reflect on the transitions taking place in themselves as they undertake this life-changing journey.

OUTLINE OF THIS BOOK

In Part One we travel across the sacred lands of the ancient near east and approach five significant river systems.

We begin with the rivers flowing from Eden, the Euphrates and Tigris. We learn how today their waters are hoarded and not equitably shared. This leads us, as we turn to the biblical accounts, to learn about big-heartedness from Abraham at the Euphrates and discover how Daniel's prophetic vocation began on the banks of the Tigris. We are challenged and heartened by six astonishing Syriac spiritual writers from the fifth and sixth centuries who lived in Mesopotamia, between the rivers.

At the Jabbok (Zarqa) river we hear how massive pollution has caused ancient peoples to move away and to question their very identity. We join Jacob in the swirling waters of the Jabbok as he discovers a new identity that will shape the self-understanding of an entire people. We'll reflect on how our identity is shaped by the waters of baptism.

We next journey into the Judean wilderness and enjoy the breathtaking beauty of the Wadi Qelt which has been identified as the Brook Cherith. We hear how in this very river valley today two peoples, often at loggerheads, represent two contrasting lifestyles, one settled and the other mobile. This focuses our attention on how action and stillness play out in the ministry of the prophet Elijah, which began on the riverbank here. We turn to those who have lived in this remarkable valley incised into the desert, Euthymius and George of Choziba: their wisdom from the fourth and seventh centuries heartens us today.

In chapter four dismay turns to hope. After learning how the once-mighty Jordan has suffered in recent years severe ecological degradation, we look at the significance of the baptism of Christ here through the lens of God opening up possibilities for the renewal of all creation. The desert fathers and mothers who lived near the Jordan model to us ways in which we can not only live in harmony with nature but even catch glimpses of a paradise restored. We are encouraged, too, by recent political commitments that promise to bring healing to these damaged waters.

The prophet Joel called the Kidron "the Valley of Decision." We recall how it became this for Jesus himself in the garden of Gethsemane, set by the brook Kidron, on the eve of his passion. The great fourth century monastic pioneer St Saba models for us creative decision-making. As we hear about the indecision which has led to the despoilment of the Kidron in recent times, we reflect on how good decision-making can take place.

In Part Two we travel to five significant wells or springs in the biblical accounts which have become the focus of pilgrimage today.

Introduction

We venture to the fringes of the Negev desert to stand beside patriarch Abraham's well, which endures here after four thousand years. At Beersheva we re-read the Genesis stories of how both Abraham and his son Isaac experienced conflict with the Philistine warlord Abimelech over wells dug and stolen. We are inspired by ancient stories of covenant-making between warring parties. As we reflect on the theme of building pathways to reconciliation in a divided world, we allow ourselves to be encouraged by the wisdom of ancient spiritual writers which speak uncannily into our own contemporary situations of conflict. In particular we consider how efforts at reconciliation can be resourced, as we ponder the phrase "We drink from our own wells."

Chapter 7 takes us to Mary's Well in noisy Nazareth. We find that it has important secrets to disclose. Mary teaches us the secret of finding God in the everyday, indeed the grace of preserving a still, contemplative heart in the very midst of needful activities. Charles de Foucauld, who lived at Nazareth for some time, helps us to look at the integration—not just co-existence—of action and contemplation, while his compatriot de Caussade opens to us the mystery of discovering the sacrament of present moment.

Like Mary (Luke 1:39) we venture next, in chapter 8, to the hill country of Judea and find ourselves standing at Ein Karem, the Spring of the Vineyard, celebrating the visitation of Mary to Elizabeth. We learn that today the village, once Arab and now Jewish, embodies the breakdown in communication between peoples. From the encounter of the two women we discover the secrets of deep and patient listening—after all, their conversation lasted three months (Luke 1:56)! From the sixteenth century founders of the Order of the Visitation, which is committed to living out this "joyful mystery" in daily life, we learn moreover how such listening can blossom into spiritual friendships and relationships marked by mutual respect and reciprocal attentiveness. The spring discloses to us the secret of speaking, and listening, with the heart.

Chapter nine takes us into the land of the Samaritans, as we join the unnamed Woman and Jesus sitting beside Jacob's Well. Before we take a fresh look at the story of John 4, we are first confronted by the brute fact that, today, the sacred Well is yards away from one of the most overcrowded refugee camps on the West Bank, Balata. It also happens to be the location of biblical Shechem, and we remind ourselves of what this meant to Abraham, Jacob and Joshua. As we are heartened by rare examples of contemporary refugees in this same setting beginning to glimpse new opportunities for human dignity amidst the squalor of today's camp, we recognize how a key theme of John 4 is that of learning to see things differently.

In our closing chapter we see how recent archaeology has massively enlarged our understanding of Jerusalem's original source of water, the Gihon spring, and the significance of the Pool of Siloam into which it first flows. These astonishing discoveries lead us to revisit the story of the healing of the man born blind (John 9) and we see, for the first time, the import of Jesus' command to him "Go and wash in the Pool of Siloam"—it is all about him rediscovering new dignity and identity as a pilgrim child of God. This takes on new poignancy as we learn of the dehumanizing and demeaning treatment meted out to current residents of Siloam (the Arab village of Silwan) today. But we close by recapturing the awesome vision of the prophet Ezekiel, who sees these waters flowing out into the desert bringing deep renewal and the healing of the nations. This reminds us that prayer and the encounter with God is the source and wellspring of our mission in the world today. Truly, the rivers and springs of the Bible, which we have discovered afresh, empower us and energize us to live lives that flow out in grace, beauty and transformative power into the deserts and wildernesses of our own time.

We might need to lament with Jeremiah:

> My people have committed two evils:
>   they have forsaken me,
> the fountain of living water,
>   and dug out cisterns for themselves,
> cracked cisterns
>   that can hold no water. (Jer 2:13)

But we will delight in Isaiah's promise:

> With joy you will draw water from the wells of salvation. (Isa 12:3)

And we'll rejoice with the Psalmist:

> There is a river whose streams make glad the city of God, the holy habitation of the Most High. (Ps 46:4)

PART ONE
Rivers of Struggle

1 Euphrates

1

EUPHRATES AND TIGRIS

Sharing Courageously

A river flows out of Eden to water the garden, and from there it divides and becomes four branches . . . The name of the third river is Tigris, which flows east of Assyria. And the fourth river is the Euphrates. (Gen 2:10–14)

WE BEGIN OUR EXPLORATION of the biblical rivers by considering together the Tigris and Euphrates: they frame Mesopotamia, crossroads of the ancient east, cradle of civilization, crucible of cultures and seedbed of saints. In this region the Christian faith flourished and many mystics lived on the riverbanks of the two rivers or their tributaries. Indeed, the Christian faith spread along the Tigris and Euphrates, aided by the routes of the Silk Road, moving downstream from Edessa and Nisibis in the north, both located on tributaries of the Euphrates.[1] Certainly there was a Christian community at Edessa by the end of the second century and it became an important catechetical center with the formation of the School of Edessa. A venerable tradition asserts that Mar Mari, one of the seventy apostles, brought the faith to Mesopotamia in the earliest times. Certainly the faith travelled

---

1. Edessa lies on the Daisan River a tributary of the Khabur, the largest perennial tributary to the Euphrates. Nisibis lies at the foot of the Mount Izla escarpment at the southern edge of the Tur Abdin hills, standing on the banks of the Jaghjagh River which flows into the Euphrates via the Khabur.

down to Nineveh (Mosul) on the Tigris, and south of Babylon and present Baghdad to Seleucia-Ctesiphon straggling the banks of the River Tigris.[2]

This land between the rivers, Mesopotamia, witnessed the flourishing of the Syriac Christian tradition, its writers and worshippers using Aramaic, the language of Jesus. We will see that they have much wisdom to share from the riverbanks that speaks both into our lives of faith, and pertinently, into the ecological crises that beset these two great biblical rivers.

TWO AWESOME RIVERS

The two rivers have their sources within 50 miles of each other in eastern Turkey and travel southeast through northern Syria and Iraq to the head of the Persian Gulf.

The Euphrates, the largest river in Southwest Asia, 1730 miles long, is formed by the confluence of two branches, the Karasu River, beginning in the historic Armenian highlands north of Erzurum, and the Murat River, issuing southwest of Mount Ararat, north of Lake Van. It descends between major ranges of the Taurus Mountains flowing through steep canyons and gorges, before progressing southeast across Syria and through Iraq. It is fed by the two tributaries of the Khabur, a major tributary originating in southeastern Turkey, and the Balikh River joining the Euphrates in eastern Syria.

The Tigris is more than a thousand miles in length. Its name means "swift river" and its snow-fed waters cascade through stunning ravines as it begins its descent from 10000 feet in the Taurus Mountains in the Armenian highlands towards the Gulf, flowing through valleys incised into plateaus before meandering across wide, flat desert-like plains. The Tigris has long been an important transport route in largely desert country: shallow-draft vessels navigate as far as Baghdad, but rafts are needed for transport upstream to Mosul. Crucially, the river brings life: it irrigates thirsty desert lands and enables flourishing agriculture with thick alluvial deposits of sediment.

ECOLOGICAL CHALLENGES

Such flourishing is under threat from two major causes: dam building in the upper reaches of the rivers and climate change.

2. Baumer, *Church of the East*. See also Rassam, *Christianity in Iraq*.

Damming and Withholding Water

Recent Turkish damming of the rivers has been the subject of deep controversy, for both its environmental effects within Turkey and its depletion of the flow of water downstream. Both the Tigris and Euphrates are experiencing drastic reductions in water flows due to Turkish hydro-engineering. Turkey's upstream control of the ebb and flow of the Tigris was advanced by its decision in 1975 to undertake the Southeast Anatolia Project (*Güneydoğu Anadolu Projesi*, GAP). An ambitious economic project motivated by national self-interest with scant regard for its effects on its neighbors, its massive dam-building scheme envisages the construction of 22 dams and 19 hydropower plants across the Tigris-Euphrates basin, encompassing ten per cent of the country's surface area. GAP aims to double Turkey's irrigable farmland but it is projected that GAP will reduce the flow of water into Iraq by approximately 80 per cent and into Syria by about 40 per cent. Tensions are soaring between the countries of the Euphrates and Tigris. Turkish President Suleyman Demirel said, "Neither Syria or Iraq can lay claim to Turkey's rivers . . . This is a matter of sovereignty. We have a right to do anything we like. The water resources are Turkey's . . . they cannot say they share our water resources."[3]

Climate Change

Turkish exploitation of the water from both the Tigris and the Euphrates has coincided with severe droughts in the region and resulted in an increasingly desperate water-shortage crisis in Iraq. This is a second cause of the ecological problems: changing climate and the potential for a permanent decrease in rainfall, together with the devastating inflow of salt water at the lower end of the river, intensify the sense of anxiety downstream on the Tigris and the potential for armed conflict. Climate change and associated droughts have had a severe impact on Iraq in recent years. According to the Cyprus Institute, Iraq and surrounding areas have already witnessed a temperature rise of 0.4°C in the past four decades, outpacing global temperature increases. The country has also faced severe droughts and heatwaves over the past years. The 2020–2021 rainfall season was the second driest in four decades, causing a reduction of water flow of 29% in the Tigris and

---

3. Daly, "Turkey's Water Policies."

73% in the Euphrates. The water flow is expected to decrease even further, by 25% and 50% respectively by the end of this year.[4]

An environmental catastrophe looms: the decrease of water volume in the lower Tigris and ending of periodic and life-giving flooding has already had devastating effects on wildlife biosystems and biodiversity. Fauna and flora are suffering due to lack of moisture.[5] Fish are dying and at Basra, for example, the polluted river water has poisoned and hospitalized many residents. Thirteen international aid groups have recently warned that the "unfolding water crisis will soon become an unprecedented catastrophe" threatening the livelihoods of over 7 million people in Iraq.[6]

Behind the two causes of impairment of the great rivers' waters lie the age-old problems of human selfishness. The hoarding of water in great reservoirs upstream and the intensification of climate change both spring from human disregard for others. How do the Biblical sources speak prophetically across the centuries to present day troubles?

COURAGE AND OPENNESS ON THE EUPHRATES

Two significant journeys across the Euphrates reveal a courage to leave the past behind and to embrace new possibilities and new adventures, and indeed, a different mindset.

Abraham

Abraham's adventures begin at Ur of the Chaldees (Gen 11:31). The current scholarly consensus for its location is in southern Mesopotamia, at Tell al-Muqayyar, 140 miles southeast of the site of Babylon and ten miles west of the present bed of the Euphrates River, located on an abandoned channel of the Euphrates River in far southern Iraq. Close by at Nasiriyah stand the remains of the ancient Ziggurat of Ur.[7]

After a sojourn at Haran, on the Balikh (the second largest tributary to the Euphrates after the Khabur) Abraham is summoned to move on again:

4. de Leth, "Tigris and Euphrates in Iraq."

5. Ayboga, "Dams in the Euphrates and Tigris Basin." See also King, *Water and Conflict*.

6. OCHA, "Water Crisis."

7. An alternative site for Ur of the Chaldees is modern Urfa on the Balikh River within the great western bend of the Euphrates.

> Now the Lord said to Abram, "Go from your country and your kindred and your father's house to the land that I will show you. I will make of you a great nation, and I will bless you, and make your name great, so that you will be a blessing. I will bless those who bless you, and the one who curses you I will curse; and in you all the families of the earth shall be blessed." So Abram went, as he Lord had told him; and Lot went with him. Abram was seventy-five years old when he departed from Haran. Abram took his wife Sarai and his brother's son Lot, and all the possessions that they had gathered, and the persons whom they had acquired in Haran; and they set forth to go to the land of Canaan. When they had come to the land of Canaan, Abram passed through the land to the place at Shechem, to the oak of Moreh. (Gen 12:1–6)

It was at Shechem that Joshua recalled this journey of the patriarch at the renewal of covenant:

> Then Joshua gathered all the tribes of Israel to Shechem, and summoned the elders, the heads, the judges, and the officers of Israel; and they presented themselves before God. And Joshua said to all the people, "Thus says the Lord, the God of Israel: Long ago your ancestors—Terah and his sons Abraham and Nahor—lived beyond the Euphrates and served other gods. Then I took your father Abraham from beyond the River and led him through all the land of Canaan and made his offspring many. I gave him Isaac; and to Isaac I gave Jacob and Esau." (Josh 24:1–4)

For Abraham the crossing of the Euphrates was the start of an astonishing journey of faith. Abraham's passage across the River represents a willingness to let go of former, inherited ways of thinking and living: it is to embrace a pilgrim heart and mind. Abraham is not stuck in his ways. He is prepared to move physically and spiritually. He is ready to welcome different vistas and new perspectives, in every sense.

Jacob

Jacob makes a similar transition and for him the Euphrates is a liminal place too, the threshold of a new future. After twenty years of servitude under his uncle Laban he is ready to embark on a journey into a new life. Jacob experienced the River as the gateway to freedom from oppression; a long journey lay ahead (we'll catch up with him in next chapter). It marked a new beginning. Like his grandfather he displayed a courage to leave past behind and move forward into the unknown:

> So Jacob arose, [from Haran] and set his children and his wives on camels; and he drove away all his livestock, all the property that he had gained, the livestock in his possession that he had acquired in Paddan-aram, to go to his father Isaac in the land of Canaan . . . So he fled with all that he had; starting out he crossed the Euphrates, and set his face toward the hill country of Gilead. (Gen 31:18–21)

GENEROSITY AND COMPASSION ON THE TIGRIS

Daniel's vision at the Tigris

> In the third year of Cyrus king of Persia, a revelation was given to Daniel. Its message was true and it concerned a great war. The understanding of the message came to him in a vision.
> At that time I, Daniel, mourned for three weeks. I ate no choice food; no meat or wine touched my lips; and I used no lotions at all until the three weeks were over. On the twenty-fourth day of the first month, as I was standing on the bank of the great river, the Tigris, I looked up and there before me was a man dressed in linen, with a belt of fine gold from Uphaz around his waist. His body was like topaz, his face like lightning, his eyes like flaming torches, his arms and legs like the gleam of burnished bronze, and his voice like the sound of a multitude. (Dan 10:1–6)

Daniel had already seen a vision of one he called Son of Man:

> I saw in the night visions,
> and behold, with the clouds of heaven there came one like a son of man,
> and he came to the Ancient of Days and was presented before him.
> And to him was given dominion and glory and kingdom,
> that all peoples, nations, and languages should serve him;
> his dominion is an everlasting dominion, which shall not pass away,
> and his kingdom one that shall not be destroyed. (Dan 7:13–14, RSV)

What effect does the vision have?

> And I, Daniel, alone saw the vision, for the men who were with me did not see the vision, but a great trembling fell upon them, and they fled to hide themselves. So I was left alone and saw this great

vision, and no strength was left in me; my radiant appearance was fearfully changed, and I retained no strength. Then I heard the sound of his words; and when I heard the sound of his words, I fell on my face in a deep sleep with my face to the ground.

And behold, a hand touched me and set me trembling on my hands and knees. And he said to me, "O Daniel, man greatly beloved, give heed to the words that I speak to you, and stand upright, for now I have been sent to you." While he was speaking this word to me, I stood up trembling. Then he said to me, "Fear not, Daniel, for from the first day that you set your mind to understand and humbled yourself before your God, your words have been heard, and I have come because of your words . . ."

When he had spoken to me according to these words, I turned my face toward the ground and was dumb. And behold, one in the likeness of the sons of men touched my lips; then I opened my mouth and spoke. I said to him who stood before me, "O my lord, by reason of the vision pains have come upon me, and I retain no strength. How can my lord's servant talk with my lord? For now no strength remains in me, and no breath is left in me."

Again one having the appearance of a man touched me and strengthened me. And he said, "O man greatly beloved, fear not, peace be with you; be strong and of good courage." And when he spoke to me, I was strengthened and said, "Let my lord speak, for you have strengthened me." (10:7–12,15–18)

What Daniel experiences on the banks of the Tigris is remarkable. The mysterious figure "like a Son of Man" gives hope and assurance in a time of deep uncertainty and insecurity. At the river Daniel feels helpless and like Moses before him protests that he cannot speak. But the Christlike Son of Man strengthens him and equips him so that at start of chapter 11 he can go to Darius and report: "I stood up to confirm and strengthen him." Daniel is equipped to be a prophet at the Tigris: he is affirmed by the "Son of Man" in his vocation, he is strengthened and emboldened. The Son of Man figure (one "in the likeness of the sons of men") is the giver of many gifts, especially courage and generosity of spirit.

The Figure From The Tigris Appears Again

Who does Daniel see in the vision at the Tigris? It sounds remarkably like the One seen by the apocalyptic seer John on the island of Patmos:

> I turned around to see the voice that was speaking to me. And when I turned I saw seven golden lampstands, and among the lampstands was someone like a son of man, dressed in a robe reaching down to his feet and with a golden sash around his chest. The hair on his head was white like wool, as white as snow, and his eyes were like blazing fire. His feet were like bronze glowing in a furnace, and his voice was like the sound of rushing waters. In his right hand he held seven stars, and coming out of his mouth was a sharp, double-edged sword. His face was like the sun shining in all its brilliance.
>
> When I saw him, I fell at his feet as though dead. Then he placed his right hand on me and said: "Do not be afraid. I am the First and the Last. I am the Living One; I was dead, and now look, I am alive for ever and ever! And I hold the keys of death and Hades." (Rev 1:12–17)

There are close links between the book of Daniel and the Revelation to St John, both being apocalyptic responses to times of extreme stress and anxious to bring reassurance. As the book of Daniel represents a courageous critique of Antioch IV Epiphanes, the Greek who desecrated the Jewish Temple in 167BC (Dan 11:31), so the Book of Revelation is a thinly-veiled critique of Roman oppression.

What is striking about the mysterious figure "like unto a Son of Man" in Daniel and the Christ figure in Revelation is that they are characterized by re-assuring generosity and a sharing of the resources they hold. In Revelation the Figure promises to those who persevere in time of stress:

- I will give permission to eat from the tree of life that is in the paradise of God (2:7)
- I will give some of the hidden manna
- I will also give the morning star (2:28)
- I will clothe you in white robes (3:5)
- I will make you a pillar in the temple of my God (3:12)
- I will give a place with me on my throne (3:21)

Later this figure will make a glorious promise about the water of life:

> See, I am making all things new. I am the Alpha and the Omega, the beginning and the end. To the thirsty I will give water as a gift from the spring of the water of life. Those who conquer will

inherit these things, and I will be their God and they will be my children. (Rev 21:5,6)

This echoes the gospel imperative:

> If you let your life go for my sake and for the sake of the gospel, you will continually experience true life. But if you choose to keep your life for yourself, you will forfeit what you try to keep. (Mark 8:35, *Passion* Translation)

> Self-help is no help at all. Self-sacrifice is the way, my way, to saving yourself, your true self. What good would it do to get everything you want and lose you, the real you? What could you ever trade your soul for? (Mark 8:35, *Message*)

Clinging to life causes life to decay, and the life that is freely given is eternal. Those who are turned in on themselves will ultimately fail. This wisdom speaks powerfully not only to those who hoard water resources on the Tigris and Euphrates today but to all who reveal a self-serving grasping attitude towards the earth's resources and who turn a deaf ear to those in need. Indeed, it speaks to all of us.

Live Wisely and Well

Daniel's experience on the banks of the Tigris ends in this way:

> As I, Daniel, took all this in, two figures appeared, one standing on this bank of the river and one on the other bank. One of them asked a third man who was dressed in linen and who straddled the river, "How long is this astonishing story to go on?"
>
> The man dressed in linen, who straddled the river, raised both hands to the skies. I heard him solemnly swear by the Eternal One that when the oppressor of the holy people was brought down the story would be complete.
>
> I heard all this plainly enough, but I didn't understand it. So I asked, "Master, can you explain this to me?"
>
> "Go on about your business, Daniel," he said. "The message is confidential and under lock and key until the end, until things are about to be wrapped up. The populace will be washed clean and made like new. Those who live wisely and well will understand what's going on." (Dan 12:5–10, *Message*)

The mysterious man clothed in linen, like the Christ figure in Revelation but now "standing over the water in the river" (NCV) appears a final time at the Tigris with an emphatic message. Ultimately, the invitation is to "live wisely and well"—for us, to live out the Gospel imperatives in a spirit of sacrificial self-giving and sharing. For the promise made to Daniel at the Tigris resounds across the centuries:

> "Men and women who have lived wisely and well will shine brilliantly, like the cloudless, star-strewn night skies. And those who put others on the right path to life will glow like stars forever." (Dan 12:3, *Message*)

VOICES FROM THE RIVERBANK

As we attend to six writers from the environs of the Tigris and the Euphrates we realize that their timeless words speak both to the causes of the present ecological crisis in these rivers and to our own lives of faith.

Aphrahat (270–346) is the author of the earliest known Syriac writings, and the first to write about prayer—in his *Demonstrations*—not confining his thoughts to a commentary on the Lord's Prayer as did former writers. He seems to have been a significant figure in the church in the Persian Empire: being selected in 344 to draw up a circular letter from a council of bishops to the churches of Ctesiphon and Seleucia on the Tigris suggests that he himself was a bishop. He developed an early spirituality of the prayer of the heart while teaching that prayer without action is useless: we must do our part as God does his. Prayer is inseparable from care, and intercession must lead to self-offering:

> Now it says in the prophet: "This is my rest; give rest to the tired" (Isa 28:12). Therefore effect this "rest" of God, and you will have no need to say "forgive me." Give rest to the weary, visit the sick, make provision for the poor: this is indeed prayer. All the time that someone effects the "rest" of God, that is prayer . . .
>
> Watch out, my beloved, lest when some opportunity of "giving rest" to the will of God meets you, you say "the time for prayer is at hand. I will pray and then act." While you are seeking to complete your prayer, that opportunity for "giving rest" will escape from you . . . Rather, effect the "rest" of God, and that will constitute prayer . . .

For our Lord said to those on his right "I was hungry and you gave me to eat. I was thirsty and you gave me to drink, I was a stranger and you welcomed me in" (Matt 25:25). Prayer is beautiful, and its works are fair; prayer is accepted when it provides alleviation, prayer is heard when forgiveness is to be found in it, prayer is effective when the power of God is made effective in it . . . Be eager in wakefulness.[8]

The Book of Steps, the earliest surviving Syriac sermons to deal with the advanced stages of growth in the spiritual life, was written anonymously at the turn of the fourth/ fifth centuries. Mention of the river Zab, a tributary of Euphrates, locates the writer in the northern part of present day Iraq. He uses the rivers as an illustration to contrast the mature and immature Christian, a key theme of his writing:

> The teacher has the right to say to one of his disciples, "Go among the tax-collectors and sinners, the wicked and the heathen" because he knows that he is a good swimmer and is able to cross over the Euphrates while it is stormy . . . He commands the other disciple, who is not able to cross over the Lesser Zaba [only a tributary of the Euphrates, in north-east Iraq] , "You should not talk with such and such a person, and you should not go to such and such a place. Beware of the tax-collectors and sinners . . . "
>
> With one disciple he speaks with love and with the other he speaks caution because he knows that this is necessary for him, as our Lord said to his disciples while they were immature, "Do not travel on the road of the Gentiles." But after they had received the Spirit of the Paraclete, he said to them, "Go among the Gentiles . . . ," just as Jesus went among the tax-collectors and sinners.[9]

Jacob of Serug (451–521) was one of the best Syriac poets. Like Ephrem (306–373) before him, he held a deeply sacramental approach to creation and saw symbols of the Divine everywhere. Born at Kurtam, a village on the Euphrates to the west of Harran, and probably educated at Edessa, he described himself to God:

> I am Your flute: breathe into me Your Spirit, O Son of God.
> Let me give forth melodies filled with wonder . . .
> May Your power move me, as wind moves a reed and sings thereby
> a sweet song in a loud sound . . .

---

8. Brock, *Syriac Fathers*, 20,21.
9. Kitchen and Parmentier, *Book of Steps*, 351, 352.

> Through You, O Lord, through the mouth be moved to bring forth
> new melodies, full of wonder,
> singing praises without disharmony.[10]
> I am a ten-stringed harp that You have fashioned:
> Pluck me that I may play for Your glory, yes on account of You!
> Strum me with Your finger and strum my silent strings . . .
> A harp cannot give melody of its own accord,
> And unless its player plucks it, it remains mute and silent . . .
> Play me, O my Master, for You hold me and I behold You;
> Inspire in me rich praise concerning Your manifestation!
> The string is my soul, and behold, it is silent without Your
> glorification![11]

Perhaps he had in mind the primordial Euphrates that flowed past him when he wrote:

> O Fountain of Life from which the dead drank and became alive (Ps 6:9),
> pour Yourself into me and quench my thirst from Your fountain.
> O Drink that flowed into the thirsty earth and it produced fruit,
> let me drink from You and I shall call out openly how sweet You are . . .
> O Son of God who called Himself "Living Water,"
> give me to drink and when I shall be satiated by You,
> let me speak about You.
> O Fountain which from the beginning
> descended from the height to the earth,
> With Your drink let my mind bring forth fruits of praise to Your Father.[12]

He delights in the compassion and generosity of God and longs for a return to Eden:

> Come, You who are not distant in giving each day
> all kinds of good things
> to the person who seeks to receive freely
> the wealth that comes from You.
> You are close by, O Son of God, You are close at hand
> to grant each day all kinds of requests for those who ask.
> You are close by, and here You are, with us Emmanuel;
> You have wearied Yourself by bringing blessings and riches
> for the entire world . . .
> Mercy mingled You with humanity, so that You might save it.
> You scattered Your treasures over the poor and made them rich,

10. Harvey, "Jacob of Serug," 17–18.
11. Hansbury, *Prayers*, 71, 72.
12. Hansbury, *Prayers*, 43.

the dead came to life in You,
and the world that had become corrupted was set in order....
You came down like rain upon the lands that lay waste,
You made them like Paradise full of blessings...
Adam was renewed in You,
and returned to Eden which he had lost.[13]

John of Dalyatha (690–c.780), also known John Saba ("the Elder") and as John the Venerable, was a monk and mystic of the Church of the East. John was born in the village of Ardamut, northeast of Mosul in the Syriac-speaking region of Beth Nuhadra, part of the Syrian province of the Umayyad Caliphate between the Khabur River and the Tigris. He became a monk on the border of present day Iraq/ Turkey and alternated between coenobitic (community-based) and eremitic (solitary) monasticism, with a preference for the latter, enjoying the solitude of the 9,000 feet high mountains of Dalyatha, north of Qardu. At the time of his death, he was serving as the abbot of a community of monks. He writes:

> Blessed are you who always satisfy your soul with living waters,
> the drinkers of which do not die, for they flow from the fount of blessings, which is Christ the splendor of the Father...
> Happy the one whose thoughts are silenced by the thought of you
> O God, for the Spirit causes rivers of life to well up in that person for their own delight and for those who thirst for a vision of you.[14]

Joseph the Visionary was born (c.710) into a Zoroastrian family, and at the age of seven he was taken captive in a raid, and sold as a slave, first to an Arab in Sinjar, and then to a Christian in the Qardu area. Impressed by the life of the monks at the monastery of John of Kamul, he sought baptism. Liberated by his owner, he became a monk in Beth Nuhadra near the headwaters of the Tigris. In a remarkable passage, Joseph writes that as prayer progresses, we develop an increasing capacity for compassion:

> A sign of the operation of the Spirit in you is the mercifulness that fashions within you the image of God, so that when your thought is extended to all people, tears are shed from your eyes like fountains of water. It is as if people are all dwelling in your heart, and you lovingly embrace and kiss them, pouring your kindness over them all in your thought. Whenever you remember them your heart is kindled by the power of the Spirit working in you like a

13. Hansbury, *Prayers*, 59–61.
14. Colless, *Pearlers*, 161, 165.

fire. This engenders in your heart goodness and kindness, so you cannot bring yourself to speak any unkind thing to any person, nor does your imagination think evil of anyone, but you do good to all, in thought and deed.[15]

Isaac of Nineveh (613–700) develops this big-heartedness even further. Sojourning on the banks of the Tigris for a season as bishop of Nineveh, before retiring to the mountains of Khuzistan for solitude and the teaching of monks, Isaac teaches us about God's all-embracing love: every creature is precious in God's sight.

Isaac encourages us to leave behind small ideas of God. He notices that we project onto God our own human ideas of justice, vengeance and retribution, but these are an insult to God and reveal tiny-mindedness. We should not limit God to our own narrow categories or squeeze him into a mold of our own making. Isaac is quite clear that we should quit infantile ideas about God (2/XXXIX:14).[16] In the course of his meditative prayer, Isaac discovers an overwhelming sense of God's mercy and how much God cherishes each individual. We are precious and he does not inflict punishment on us. This shapes Isaac's whole approach to the question of "Gehenna"—hell. Such a state after death must, understands Isaac, be a temporary place marked by repentance, healing, purgation. Why would God create people only to have them condemned forever? God's foreknowledge of human proclivities must exclude the imposition of eternal punishment which, says Isaac, is totally incompatible with the God of love. He is principally loving Father not exacting Judge.

Isaac's vision of *apocatastasis* is the ultimate restoration of creation to a condition of perfection, the renewal of all things and all people, including a fractured and despoiled planet. It is an echo of Paul's ideas in Romans 8:18–24. For Isaac,

> Everyone has a single place in His purpose in the ranking of love, corresponding to the form He beheld in them before He created them . . . He has a single ranking of complete and impassible love towards everyone, and He has a single caring concern for those who have fallen, just as much as for those who have not fallen. (2/XL:3)

---

15. Colless, *Pearlers*, 146.

16. See Mayes, *Diving for Pearls*. Extracts from Wensinck, *Mystical Treatises* are cited, for example, as 1/ XX: 109. Extracts from the newly-discovered *Second Part* by Isaac of Nineveh are cited, for example, as 2/ X: 32.

"In every epoch," Alfeyev writes, "the Christian world needs to be reminded of this universal love of God for his creation because in every epoch there is a strong tendency within Christianity to replace the religion of love and freedom taught by Jesus with a religion of slavery and fear."[17]

Isaac has stumbled on a great discovery and an insight that will shape his entire writing and ministry and he shares it with daring and confidence:

> Among all His actions there is none which is not entirely a matter of mercy, love and compassion: this constitutes the beginning and the end of His dealings with us ... How much to be worshipped is our Lord God's gentle compassion and His immeasurable munificence. (2/XXXIX:22)

His conviction that the Kingdom of God triumphs over Gehenna and his sense of God's compassion emerge from Isaac's profound mystical experience. He is offering us a paradigm shift and a fresh vision of God's grace. This is subversive wisdom that calls into question traditional views of divine retribution. Isaac is pushing the boundaries of our understanding of God's care for humanity and of God's commitment to humanity. His teaching springs from the deep place of prayer, from the embrace of God that he has himself experienced in solitude and stillness. His encounter with God becomes transformative—shattering inherited ideas about God and opening up new vistas of grace. In a sentence:

> There exists with God a single love and compassion which is spread out over all creation, a love which is without alteration, timeless and everlasting. (2/XL:1)

ALL-EMBRACING CARE

We have seen how the Biblical stories associated with the Euphrates show us Abraham and Jacob moving out in faith and utter openness. They are prepared to change their mind and embrace a different future as they step forward from the Euphrates. We have seen that Daniel's encounter at the Tigris with a figure "like unto a Son of Man" empowers him to accept the vocation of a prophet and leads him to glimpse the generosity and providence of God. The voices from the riverbank, in their different ways, urge us to a kind of prayer that leads to action. These perspectives speak powerfully

---

17. Alfeyev, *Legacy*, 300–301.

to present-day temptations to selfishness on the great rivers. And if God's love is so all-embracing, as Isaac of Nineveh discovers, then above all we too should seek a compassionate heart:

> What is a merciful heart? It is the heart's burning for the sake of the entire creation, for people, for birds, for animals, for demons and for every created thing; and by the recollection and sight of them the eyes of a merciful one pour forth abundant tears. From the strong and vehement mercy which grips our heart and from our great compassion, our heart is humbled and we cannot bear to hear or see any injury or slight sorrow in creation. For this reason we continually offer up tearful prayer, even for irrational beasts, for the enemies of the truth and for those who harm us, that they be protected and receive mercy. And in like manner we even pray for the family of reptiles because of the great compassion that burns in our heart without measure in the likeness of God. (1/LXXIV:341)

QUESTIONS FOR REFLECTION

1. One emerging theme of this chapter is listening to God and taking responsibility for a new course of action. How do you find yourself reacting to the experiences of Abraham and Jacob?

2. In what ways might you identify with Daniel as he stands on the banks of the Tigris?

3. What situations of selfishness or hoarding come to mind as you read of the double trouble facing the Euphrates and Tigris today? How can you respond courageously and with generosity of spirit?

4. Which Syriac spiritual writer here challenges you or heartens you the most? Why?

5. Ponder the words of Psalm 137, the song of the exiles besides the river Tigris.

> By the rivers of Babylon – there we sat down and there we wept
> when we remembered Zion.
> On the willows there we hung up our harps.
> For there our captors asked us for songs,
> and our tormentors asked for mirth,
> saying, "Sing us one of the songs of Zion!"
> How could we sing the Lord's song in a foreign land?

Euphrates And Tigris

> If I forget you, O Jerusalem, let my right hand wither!
> Let my tongue cling to the roof of my mouth,
> if I do not remember you,
> if I do not set Jerusalem above my highest joy.

What harps might you have to hang up beside the river? Is there a regret or a loss that you need to decisively let go of?

Jacob Wrestling with the Angel, Gustave Doré (1855)

2

JABBOK

Struggling For Identity

That night Jacob got up and crossed the ford of the Jabbok (Gen 32:22)

FROM TIME IMMEMORIAL RIVERS have shaped the identity and destiny of peoples. They have molded cultures and forged civilizations. Rivers influence the health and well being of people, their livelihoods and occupations, their very survival. Many people define themselves in relation to a river. For example, the Bible describes the people of the Holy Land as living between the River (Jordan in east) and the Sea (Mediterranean in west), or between Dan (river in north) and Beersheva (place of wells in south).[1] Today those who live in the areas north and south of Jerusalem dwell in an area called the West Bank—of the Jordan River. Galileans are those who live in proximity to the Sea of Galilee, which names an entire region.

In ways large and small, our surroundings shape our lives. Our productivity, happiness, and creativity are all functions of place: where we are affects who we are.

---

1. See 2 Sam 17:11.

JABBOK'S PAST

A River-shaped Identity

The Jabbok (meaning "luxuriant river" in Hebrew), after rising at Amman, makes a wide circuit, flowing first to the east, then to the northwest, until it is joined by the stream from Wadi Jerash, then westward, and flows, with many windings, down to the Jordan. The length of the river is about 60 miles. It drains a wider area than any other stream east of the Jordan, except the Yarmuk. The bed of the river is in a deep gorge with steep, precipitous banks. It cuts a great cleft, dividing the historic land of Gilead in two. For millennia it has been a thicky wooded valley, lined along its course in the past by a luxuriant growth of oleander which lit up the valley with brilliant color.

The headwaters of the Jabbok tell the story of peoples whose very identity was shaped by the riverine environment. A road-building project in the 1990s led to the discovery of a Neolithic community at Ain Ghazal—the "spring of the gazelle," one of the sources of the Jabbok on the edge of present-day Amman. Here, on the banks of the Jabbok ten millenia ago mobile hunter-gatherers began to settle in a village sustained by farming and herding—and remarkable artefacts from this period have been found.[2] In 1200 BC the Ammonites established their capital, Rabbath Ammon, alongside the source of the Jabbok—indeed 2 Samuel 12:27 calls it "the city of waters." This location made it ideal as the royal city which drew its wealth from well-watered agricultural surroundings and from international trade conducted along the main north–south road of the Transjordanian highlands—the "King's Highway." As a border city, Rabbath-Ammon lay in the path of the caravan trade between Arabia and the major centers of the Fertile Crescent and became a hub for nomadic tribes who lived by raising sheep, goats, and camels.

From ancient times the Jabbok has been a key element in the self-definition of peoples. The Jabbok was the northern boundary of the territory of Sihon the Amorite (Num 21:24). The Ammonites settled along the upper and central Jabbok River and in the area of its tributaries. Their eastern border was the desert, with the central Jabbok constituting their northern boundary (Deut 3:16; Josh 12:2).

Successive occupations—Assyrians, Babylonians, Persians, Greeks, Romans and Moslems—all formed riparian communities clustered by

---

2. Wikipedia, "Ayn Ghazal (archaeological site)."

springs like Ain Ghazal. In the 1860s, under the rule of the Ottomans, Circassian tribes, Moslems escaping religious prosecution from Russia, settled on the ancient site of Rabbath Ammon, especially around seasonal streams feeding the Jabbok: their riverine livelihood depended on cultivation on both sides of the streams. The town became Amman, and capital of the new state of TransJordan and later, of the Kingdom of Jordan, swollen by thousands of Palestinian refugees in 1948 and 1967. Amman's population has grown from 2000 in the 1920s to 3 million. The river's watershed encompasses the most densely populated areas east of the Jordan River.

As we approach the waters of the Jabbok, we see that the search for identity and self-confidence becomes a recurring theme.

JABBOK'S PRESENT

River of Blue?

The Jabbok is called *Nahr ez-Zarqa* in Arabic, meaning "river of blue" and referring to the clear blue color of its water—but in recent times this has become a misnomer, for its color now is brown due to effluent and human waste. The continuous deterioration of the river's ecosystem over decades is the one of the biggest environmental challenges in Jordan.[3]

The Zarqa/Jabbok river is highly polluted. In many areas, raw sewage flows untreated directly into the river through dry riverbeds, contaminating it and creating an appalling stench, particularly during the summer months. Noxious input desecrates the river. Sewage treatment stations have been built in two locations (including Ain Ghazal and Khirbet As Samra), but untreated water overflows directly to the Zarqa river. The poor condition of the river is exacerbated by illegal dumping of industrial waste and oils from garages. It is being poisoned by toxic chemicals. Environmental degradation in the Zarqa River is devastating ecosystems with a loss of biodiversity, killing scarce vegetation cover, spreading disease among humans and livestock, and increasing poverty and degrading livelihood conditions. This vulnerable ecosystem has been subjected to many changes and disturbances during the past 50 years: over-extraction of underground water has led to the desiccation of surface vegetation while soil erosion from

---

3. Union Internationale pour la Conservation de la Nature, "Zarqa River Basin Restoration."

overgrazing and the cropping of marginal lands has been compounded by the encroachment of urban development into natural habitats.[4]

Pollutants released to the Zarqa River have been identified, quantified, and linked to their sources. The methodology included field observation of the river and chemical analysis of samples. However until recently, more attention has been given to scientific data about water degradation than to noticing how the self-confidence and identity of riverine people has been eroded or contaminated. In 2018 a major conference in Brisbane identified the pressing need for attending to this dimension:

> River flows connect people, places, and other forms of life, inspiring and sustaining diverse cultural beliefs, values, and ways of life. The concept of environmental flows provides a framework for improving understanding of relationships between river flows and people, and for supporting those that are mutually beneficial. Nevertheless, most approaches to determining environmental flows remain grounded in the biophysical sciences. The 2018 Brisbane Declaration and Global Action Agenda on Environmental Flows represents a new phase in environmental flow science and an opportunity to better consider the co-constitution of river flows, ecosystems, and society, and to more explicitly incorporate these relationships into river management. We synthesize understanding of relationships between people and rivers as conceived under the renewed definition of environmental flows.[5]

The journal *Frontiers in Environmental Science* noted

> The intangible spiritual attachments between people, rivers and wetlands are enduring, and the human inclination to revere rivers and celebrate symbols and rituals relating to water is universal. Many human societies ascribe meaning to water and its flow, transmitting shared understandings of the world through cultural objects and practices, including ecosystem protection. Managing environmental water sustainably is necessary to protect and restore these natural and cultural heritage values.[6]

---

4. Al-Omari et al. "Pollution Sources to Zarqa River."
5. Anderson, "Understanding Rivers."
6. Arthington et al, "Environmental Flows."

Identity Threatened

The Jabbok river not only sculpts the contours of the landscape but shapes the identity and self-understanding of communities. Alongside the Jabbok, the residents were a river people who fished in the river, and washed in it and drank from it. It was the source of their life and watered their plantings for food. It shaped their very lives. Today they can no longer relate to it in a wholesome sense, for it has become a source of disease and in parts, an open sewer. No community has been more affected by the environmental degradation than the Bedouin. For millennia Bedouin tribes have enjoyed a nomadic pattern of life, living in black tents and moving their herds along the rivers and, in desert places, from well to well. Theirs was a sustainable lifestyle that honored the natural resources of land and water.

New international borders have severed pastoral routes, and the cement blockhouse has replaced the goat-wool tent. This shift from pastoralism to sedentary lifestyle and land use of the Bedouin tribes has become widespread in Jordan; there are only few places in the country where the traditional lifestyle of Bedouin tribes survives. The 1952 Census, when the population of Amman stood at 250,000, some 29 per cent of the population were living in tents, and a further 8 per cent were dwelling in natural caves: today the number is a fraction of this. There are still Bedouin families who use tents and still move from area to area seeking grass for their livestock, but many now have houses and work in the civil services, army and schools. There are several factors at play: government policy has encouraged the settlement of Bedouin, while the perilous state of the rivers and water sources has made their ancient way of life untenable. The waters are now challenging the Bedouin to reassess their very vocation on lands they have traversed for millennia and shift into a revised understanding of their very identity.[7]

The Jordanian government has plans for rehabilitation of the Zarqa/Jabbok basin, inching towards the top of priorities of environmental management in Jordan. But progress in this complex and costly challenge is painfully slow.

---

7. Raheb, *Shifting Identities*. See also Lewis, *Multiple Identities*.

IDENTITY DISCOVERED AT THE JABBOK

The Exodus

In the biblical narratives of the closing stages of the Exodus journey the crossing of the Jabbok prompts the Hebrew nomads towards a new sense of their identity. In the long trek towards the promised land Moses realizes that he needs to cross the Jabbok:

> Then Israel sent messengers to King Sihon of the Amorites, saying, "Let me pass through your land; we will not turn aside into field or vineyard; we will not drink the water of any well; we will go by the King's Highway until we have passed through your territory." But Sihon would not allow Israel to pass through his territory. Sihon gathered all his people together, and went out against Israel to the wilderness; he came to Jahaz, and fought against Israel. Israel put him to the sword, and took possession of his land from the Arnon to the Jabbok, as far as to the Ammonites. (Num 21:21–24 cf. Judg 11:19)

Moses found this region to be full of threats—personified in Sihon King of the Ammonites and Og the King of Bashan. However God promises Moses that it will be possible to negotiate the formidable barrier of the Jabbok (Deut 3:16–17).

As they crossed the Jabbok and approached the Jordan, for the Israelites these rivers changed from being barriers to being crossing-places, and locus of fundamental transition. Here the people experienced a profound reshaping of their identity. They had been refugees and slaves, escaping from Pharaoh's tyranny in Egypt. Homeless nomads were becoming residents in a territory they cherished. Scholars consider that the designation "Hebrew" derives from the concept of the *Habiru*, which denotes an inferior, landless, shifting population, without a name or identity.[8] Their self-understanding had been shaped by the saying "Our father Abraham was a wandering Aramean" (Deut 26:5). But as they approached the Jordan no-bodies were becoming somebodies. In this passage through the waters of the Jabbok and subsequently the Jordan something was shifting in the soul of the people: there was an inner journey taking place, as well as an outer. They were gaining a new dignity and a new future. Their wilderness wanderings were drawing to an end. Now an entirely new phase of their existence beckoned.

8. Redmount, "Bitter Lives."

There are two accounts of the advent in about 1250BC into the territory in the Hebrew Scriptures: the idealized narrative of the Book of Joshua tells of a fast and dramatic takeover of the land under Joshua's leadership, a mighty invasion and conquest achieved by the destruction of the locals, but the Book of Judges suggests a more gradual migration and infiltration of a people who need to co-exist with its indigenous inhabitants. In the time of the Judges ongoing conflicts over the Jabbok took place (Judg 11:4-6, 12-13).

Judges and Kings

The River Jabbok was witness to many struggles—not only in the time of Moses and the Judges who sought to consolidate Israelite presence in this valley and its environs in Gilead, but also in the time of Saul (against Ammonite king Nahash) and David (against his son Hanun), a period marked by ongoing conflicts with the Arameans and Ammonites in the region of the Jabbok, as told in the books of Samuel and Chronicles. All these struggles involved in some way the question of identity—as Israelites sought to clarify at the same time their self-understanding as a people and the extent of the territories which might make up the Promised Land. But if we are to learn from the Jabbok river something about the search for identity, we must go back into the earliest period of the Patriarchs.

STRUGGLING AT THE JABBOK

The most fundamental and crucial question which faces each person is "Who am I?" "How can I be sure that God loves me?" These are precisely the questions raised by the figure of Jacob in his struggle related in Genesis 32:22-31. This tale has touched the hearts and minds of people from time immemorial because it echoes the experience of humanity in every age. Like the story of Adam and Eve, it can be read as a parable that deals with basic issues of life itself. It is an archetypal tale, for it represents the struggle of everyone.

It is the struggle of all humanity with God. Jacob wrestled and fought with a Stranger, an unknown figure. We never learn their name, but Jacob later described this encounter as saying "I have seen God face to face." It was indeed a divine-human combat.

Jacob is truly a representative figure in this story. First, he stands for the Jewish people. He is given the name "Israel," with an explanation that this means "one who struggles with God." The very name which comes to denote the Chosen People affirms the place of struggling with God. Jacob, son of Isaac and grandson of Abraham, is a "patriarch," a founding father of the nation. He personifies the people of Israel. As Old Testament scholar Gerhard von Rad writes about this story:

> It contains experiences of faith that extend from the most ancient period down to the time of the narrator; there is charged to it something of the entire divine history into which Israel was drawn . . . as it is now related it is clearly transparent as a type of that which Israel experienced from time to time with God. Israel has here presented its entire history with God almost prophetically as such a struggle until the breaking of the day.[9]

But the figure of Jacob in this tale also represents the Christian. Paul calls the Church "the new Israel" and insists that we are the children and offspring of Abraham. So, we can truly see ourselves in Jacob and recognize our struggles in his.

The ancient story of Genesis 32 contains seven symbolic elements that we will explore. In language which is evocative, enigmatic, and elusive, it speaks across the centuries to our own experience.

The Journey: "The Same Night He Arose.."

The life of Jacob depicted in Genesis is the story of a person in search of their identity. Jacob found it very hard to accept that God loved him, for himself as an individual, and that God wanted him for God's self. The struggle at the Jabbok River was the culmination of a life of trying to come to terms with the reality of God.

In a sense the journey begins when Jacob emerges from Rebeccah his mother's womb, clutching the heel of his elder twin born seconds before him (Gen. 25.26). From his first moment Jacob grows up in the shadow of Esau. He seems to be continually overshadowed by Esau who is his father's favorite. In an age when honor and privilege went to the first-born son, Jacob feels intimidated and suffers some kind of inferiority complex. His life is marked by fierce rivalry and competition. He comes to see himself

---

9. von Rad, *Genesis*.

JABBOK

as a second best and resorts to deception and deviousness to get the upper hand. Twice Jacob tricks his brother. He gets him to sell his birthright, his privileges as the elder son, for a single meal (25.3). Later when his blind father Isaac wishes to solemnly impart his blessing and the guarantee of inheritance, Jacob pretends to be Esau. Jacob cannot accept that God has plans for his own life, so he tries to advance himself. Lacking faith and trust in God, Jacob takes a path of stubborn self reliance. But after robbing Esau of his rightful blessing, Jacob must flee to escape his brother's vengeance. This journey represents Jacob's quest for identity, his personal search to make something of his life in his own right.

He travels hundreds of miles from the south of Canaan to Haran in the far north (near today's Turkish/Syrian border). He settles with distant relatives and is shamefully mistreated by his uncle Laban who exacts 20 years' service from him in return for the promise of his daughter Rachel in marriage. This is a time of painful exile for Jacob, far from his parents' home. It is his turn to be duped and cheated by others. But after Rachel bears him the gift of a son, Jacob knows it is time to return home. He is pursued by angry Laban who cannot let go of his daughters. A long and tiresome trek south brings Jacob into the area where he will expect to encounter his estranged brother Esau. Jacob is eaten up with anxiety and fear as he realizes, he must pass into Esau's territory. He devises a plan to appease Esau with a substantial gift. His past is catching up with him once again, and his future stretches ahead of him: but first he must cross the waters of the Jabbok. Jacob arrives at the Jabbok weary and conscious of his own failings and fears. He has manipulated others and suffered abuse himself. He is vulnerable—and also ready for an encounter with God.

We can identify with Jacob in several ways. In our life's journey we also get bruised and disenchanted with others. God gives us, like Jacob, the freedom and the space to make our own mistakes. God's gift of freewill allows us to shape our own destiny and make our own choices. Like Jacob, we can find it hard to believe God is really interested in our own life. The vital thing is that we allow our pains and fears and hurts to pass over into an encounter with God.

In today's technological and computerized world, which often fosters a sense of anonymity and impersonality, we need to rediscover our true worth in God's eyes. Like Jacob, we can lose perspective on our spiritual journey about our true dignity. We need to learn, as he was to learn at the

Jabbok River, that our real value comes not from what others might say about us, but from what God has to say about us...

Jacob kept moving in his journey and when he came face to face with God, he brought with him all his insecurities. He did not seek to evade God. At times in our own journey, we too may feel insignificant, insecure. Yet God is waiting for us in the waters. God is beckoning us to move into them, just as we are.

Reaching the Frontier: "He Crossed the Ford of the Jabbok"

The Jabbok ford is close to the Jordan, and forms part of the boundary of Canaan, the promised land. It represents a threshold into the future, the possibility of a new beginning. In more than one sense it represents a limit. Jacob has reached the limit of his own resources. He has grasped and schemed and tried by his own cleverness to gain success. Now he stands on the brink of discovering that God longs for him. The Jabbok represents a frontier—the line that marks the edge of his capabilities also marks the start, the fringes of the promised land, the land of freedom.

Jacob could have viewed the Jabbok in more negative terms. It could have become for him a barrier –a place to halt and go no further. But he realizes that the river, though a place of potential danger, is essentially a ford, a crossing-over place, a way to get from one territory to another. It represents for us a place of transition, where God calls us courageously to face new possibilities. Encounter with God can be a risky business. But it can also enable us in our life to cross boundaries—by letting go of the past, we can embrace a new future.

From Jacob's vantage point, he could also see far ahead. Before him lay the great rift valley of the Jordan, and beyond it, through the mists rising from the Dead Sea, he could make out in the distance, the first craggy mountains of Canaan, the land of promise. To come to a true sense of our identity, we sometimes need to look away from our ourselves and recapture a sense of the Otherness of God, the horizon beyond which we cannot see. Things start to take on a new perspective when we place ourselves in the larger picture. Too often, we are the center of our own universe. Like Jacob, we need to see horizons once again, which beckon us to move beyond ourselves and which remind us that God is there, in our future.

Before Jacob stretched a vast panorama, a vista stretching many miles. It calls to mind lines from Frederick Faber's great hymn:

> There's a wideness in God's mercy like the wideness of the sea . . .
> For the love of God is broader than the measures of man's mind . . .
> But we make God's love too narrow by false limits of our own
> And we magnify God's strictness with a zeal God will not own.

Passing through the Waters: "Across the Stream . . ."

Jacob's struggle with God takes place in the depths of the river Jabbok, the place where travelers pass over. There is a splashing and scrambling amidst the swirling currents. The account has echoes of the opening verses of Genesis: "the earth was a formless void, and darkness covered the face of the deep, while a wind from God swept over the face of the waters." The Bible opens with a picture of primordial chaos in the waters. The waters are the place where God begins God's creation. Even more significantly, to the readers of Genesis, the waters flowing through the Jabbok evoke of the memory of the Exodus. The waters have become a powerful symbol of liberation for the people of Israel, recalled each Passover. Moses led his people through the Red Sea to freedom, escaping slavery and oppression of Egypt, and the waters flooded back and drowned the enemy pursuing them.

For Christian readers, the waters of the Jabbok recall of the experience of Baptism. For Christians, the waters of Baptism are a place of death and resurrection effecting a dying to self, a dying to the old way of life. Our rising from the water marks a sharing in Christ's resurrection and in the newness of life that Christ brings. This is the Christian "passover," the passing from death to new life.

Though Baptism is a once and for all event, we have to return to the waters, as we do in worship each Easter. We have to make our own, again and again, the victory of Baptism. We have to go back to the waters and struggle and fight again and again as we seek to break through to new triumphs in Christian journey. For Christians, all spirituality is *paschal*—that is, marked by the Easter mystery of death and resurrection. Augustine said, "We are a Easter people and Alleluia is our song."

Let us allow this image of Jacob grappling with God in the splashing waters to speak to us of our daily struggle to enter in to all that Baptism signifies. All our life we will be struggling in the waters to make a reality—this dying to sin and selfishness and rising to newness of life. All our life God will be calling us to enter more fully into the Easter mystery, to appropriate it and make it our own ever more deeply. It is better not to hover on the brink of the river and avoid this struggle. God invites us to take the plunge, to step into the waters and to meet God face to face. The swirling waters represent the place of struggling with God, but it is here that liberation and re-creation will be experienced.

Alone with God: "Jacob Was Left Alone..."

We must have space in our prayers for solitude if we are to encounter God deeply. For Jacob this meant a letting go, for the moment, of attachments to people and possessions. He was prepared to part from family and to stand alone.

Solitude is an essential element in a spirituality of struggle. We must make time and find a place where we can be real with God. The Desert Fathers of the fourth century went out into the wilderness to seek God. They found the desert to be a place of truth. It was like entering a state of spiritual nakedness before God, where masks drop off end there is no place to hide.

To be alone with God is not easy. It is demanding and it is risky. Jacob did not know what to expect but he sensed he had to cross the ford entirely alone. If we are to meet with God, we must be ready to stop hiding behind fine-sounding prayers and holy books. All these "props" can become barriers to God, ways of evading a direct encounter with God. Rather we need the courage to come before God and honestly expose to God our heart's longings and fears. To enter solitude is to come to a place of vulnerability and utter openness to God. Henri Nouwen put it: "Solitude is thus the place of purification and transformation, the place of the great struggle and the great encounter. Solitude is the place where Christ remodels us in Christ's own image and frees us from the victimizing compulsions of the world. Solitude is the place of salvation."[10]

Solitude is, above all, the place where we can learn to *receive* from God. All his life, Jacob was used to making it on his own, and striving by his own schemes to get his way with God. In his experience of solitude at the Jabbok, Jacob would discover that blessing comes from God, not by his own efforts, but by clinging to God in the silence. This is a real problem for Christians today, taught by the world to get results by working hard, by achieving. Targets of productivity are set, and pressures mount, for rewards are dependent on what we can do. But this is a timeless issue too—was not the major debate of the Reformation in the sixteenth century precisely

10. Nouwen, *Way of the Heart*, 31.

over this issue—whether we reach God through our *own* works or through God's gift of grace?

The problem is, we are not very good at receiving from God. We would rather *do* something. Solitude teaches us the hard lesson—give up trying to achieve all the time. Start receiving.

Entering the Darkness: "And a Man Wrestled with Jacob until the Breaking of the Day."

Jacob's struggle with the divine Stranger takes place in the darkness. It is night. It was John of the Cross who coined the phrase "the dark night of the soul." This fifteenth century Spanish mystic gave three reasons for using this image to describe aspects of the spiritual journey. First, says John, in the dark we cannot actually see. In the deeper reaches of prayer, we need to shut down our five senses because they hold us captive in a state of attachment to the material world and activate our self-seeking appetites. Secondly, in the dark we cannot easily make out obstacles or turnings along the path, so we must move forward in trust. "We walk by faith, not by sight." In our relationship with God, we must take the risk of moving forwards without knowing the precise route. We venture into the unknown. Thirdly, John says, the darkness speaks of God as Mystery. God is not something we can box in and neatly label—God is quite beyond our best concepts and categories. But "the dark night of the soul" is not for John a negative experience, but rather a time of growth and healing. In his great poem he writes:

> O guiding night!
> O night more lovely than the dawn!
> O night that has united
> the Lover with his beloved,
> transforming the beloved in her Lover!"[11]

The night, for John, and for Jacob, is a place of transformation. It represents a time when we allow God to do God's work powerfully within us, reshaping and redirecting our Ego, and leading us into a greater surrender to the Divine.

Many spiritual writers in fact use the image of "darkness" to speak of entering into the mysterious presence of God. The English fourteenth century author of the *Cloud of Unknowing* puts it like this:

---

11. Kavanaugh and Rodriguez, *St John of the Cross*.

> When you first begin, you find only darkness, and as it were, a cloud of unknowing. You don't know what this means except that in your will you feel a simple steadfast intention reaching out towards God . . . Reconcile yourself to wait in this darkness as long as is necessary, but still go on longing after the One whom you love. For if you are to feel God or to see God in this life, it must always be in this cloud, in this darkness.[12]

The experience of darkness in our spiritual life can be bewildering, unsettling, and even threatening. But we can see it as a time for healing and truthful encounter with God. It is precisely in this darkness that Jacob receives unspeakable blessing. But not before he is wounded by God.

The Wounding

"When the Man saw that he did not prevail against Jacob, he touched the hollow of his thigh; and Jacob's thigh was put out of joint as he wrestled with him . . . The sun rose upon him as he passed Peniel, limping because of his thigh."

Jacob is brought to a point of brokenness. He had, it seems, often been on the run—running away from Esau and fleeing to the far north, running from Laban who chased him from Haran, and running from God—always avoiding facing up to God, evading opportunities to bring to God his true feelings and failures. Now Jacob can run no longer. His running had been symbolic both of his desire to escape uncomfortable truths and conflicts, and of his desire to stay in control of his life. He would go where he wished to go, and no one would stop him.

Now he can only limp. God touches him and disables him. He is reduced to a state of new dependence on God's very self. This wounding of Jacob represents God finally melting his stubbornness, willfulness and self-centeredness. For the moment, at least, he crumples up. He loses control. God has the mastery. God paralyses his defiant, independent Ego.

In his poems and in his prose, John of the Cross, speaks often of God's "wound of love": "You have wounded me in order to cure me, O divine hand!" The pain of the "dark night," according to John, is the costly lowering of our "defense mechanisms" before the living God. We have self-protective strategies that try to keep God at a safe distance –where he cannot disturb us too much! We fence ourselves off to protect ourselves from too-close an

---

12. Wolters, *Cloud of Unknowing*, 53.

involvement with God. But if we are to experience God in reality, we must allow ourselves to be vulnerable to God. Something has to give.

That "something" is often our desire and need to remain in control, to be at the helm of our own lives, to make our own choices, to set our own agendas. But this can be the working of a "false self" because it is denying God's grace and power. A new "Self," where God is in control, only emerges, says John, in the crucible of prayer where we allow God to burn up our rampant egotism. To return to the image of the "wounding," the pain we must face is the pain of "letting go" of being in control, the cost of being stripped of our egotistical powers. It is a bereavement, a loss.

This is a real struggle for Christians and seekers today, because it seems so contrary to the spirit of the age which exalts independent success and an "every person for themselves" mentality. Yet, paradoxically, this costly path leads to fulfilment in and through God: "For those who want to save their life will lose it—and those who lose their life for my sake and for the sake of the gospel will save it" (Mark 8.35). The word "save" here in Christ's words can be translated "heal." This fundamental dis-possession hurts but it also heals, because it restores to us a sense of wholeness, as we become the people God wants us to be, utterly surrendered to God and available to God. John Follent puts it: "The abandonment of self-mastery and the taking on of a radical dependence on God will necessarily be accompanied by a sense of being undone or being annihilated, yet such an anxiety is quite ungrounded. In fact, the discovery that one can no longer find one's guarantees in oneself may indeed be a sign that progress in the life with God is finally being achieved."[13]

Jacob moves towards wholeness in God as his pride, and self-centered stubbornness are wounded. But he also moves towards a new sense of identity.

A New Identity

"Then the Man said, "Let me go, for day is breaking." But Jacob said, "I will not let you go, unless you bless me."

Jacob, once so content to go his own way, now finds himself clinging to God. Jacob, who once sought by deceptive means to acquire blessing (deceiving his father Isaac), now cries out to God in a state of utter dependence.

---

13. Follent, "Negative Experience," 97.

This image of Jacob holding on tenaciously to God amid the splashing waters is a vivid picture of Christ's Beatitude: "Blessed are the poor in spirit—those who know their need of God—for theirs is the Kingdom of Heaven!" (Matt 5.3). The change wrought in Jacob in his struggle with God is not that overnight he will become a righteous and gracious person. Rather it is that his pride is brought low and his "Self" is surrendered to God.

And so Jacob receives the Blessing he sought—a powerful reassurance that God loves him for himself. Even more than this, God gives him a new name: "Your name shall no more be called Jacob but Israel, for you have striven with God and with humans, and have prevailed."

Jacob's experience of receiving a new name is a moment of profound affirmation by God. It declares that God *is* interested in Jacob himself. It declares that there is a uniqueness about Jacob—that God wants him for *God's very self*—that God has plans for him. This new name indicates a chosenness, a sense that God has set his love on him. The new name represents the reality that God has a singular vocation in store for each person. But what is the meaning of the new name given to Jacob in the waters of the Jabbok? Formerly, Jacob's name meant "Grasper." The new name that will come to denote a nation and will represent the people of God means "he who struggles with God."

In giving Jacob this identity God recognizes the role of struggling in an evolving relationship with him. God is declaring that it is OK to struggle with the Divine as we seek to work out who we are and what God is asking of us. The struggle is part of the spiritual journey. It is not to be avoided but faced. Indeed, in embracing our struggles with God we emerge with new strength and a clearer sense of our identity. Jacob the Grasper becomes Israel, God's warrior. Christ promises to Christians of every age: "To everyone who conquers, I will give a new name" (Rev. 2:17). In our wrestling with God we too may discover a new name for ourselves, revealed by God. If we allow God, God will hold onto us as we battle with the Divine in the waters, and affirm us as the ones God loves.

We note that Jacob seeks to uncover the identity of the One he is wrestling with: 'Then Jacob asked him, "Please tell me your name."' (32:29). But the Combatant responds: "Why is it that you ask my name?" He remains mysterious and elusive, enigmatic. Was the Stranger in the rushing waters of the Jabbok a man? An angel? Or somehow a divine figure? We never learn his name, but Jacob later described this encounter as saying "I have seen God face to face." It was indeed a divine–human combat. And it was life-changing—for Jacob has gained a new identity and the empowerment of divine blessing, which will affect his life forever. The narrative of Genesis continues: "And Jacob lifted up his eyes and looked, and behold Esau was coming" (Gen 33:1). Jacob immediately must face the brother he always had feared. He experiences a wonderful reconciliation. Then he resumes his journey and passes into the promised land: "And Jacob came safely to Shechem, which is in the land of Canaan . . . There he erected an altar and dedicated it: "to God, the God of the one who struggles" (Gen 33:20).[14]

VOICES FROM THE RIVERBANK

The Jabbok river calls us to reflect on the issue of identity. In different ways, rivers shape and reshape the terrain of our lives. In his great hymn on Genesis 32, Charles Wesley (1707–88) discovers what Jacob was unable to discover: the very name and nature of the divine Being:

> Come, O thou Traveller unknown, Whom still I hold, but cannot see!
> My company before is gone, And I am left alone with Thee;
> With Thee all night I mean to stay, And wrestle till the break of day.
>
> I need not tell Thee who I am, My misery and sin declare;
> Thyself hast called me by my name, Look on Thy hands, and read it there;
> But who, I ask Thee, who art Thou? Tell me Thy name, and tell me now.
>
> In vain Thou strugglest to get free, I never will unloose my hold!
> Art Thou the Man that died for me? The secret of Thy love unfold;
> Wrestling, I will not let Thee go, Till I Thy name, Thy nature know.
>
> Wilt Thou not yet to me reveal Thy new, unutterable Name?
> Tell me, I still beseech Thee, tell; To know it now resolved I am;
> Wrestling, I will not let Thee go, Till I Thy Name, Thy nature know.
>
> 'Tis all in vain to hold Thy tongue Or touch the hollow of my thigh;
> Though every sinew be unstrung, Out of my arms Thou shalt not fly;
> Wrestling I will not let Thee go Till I Thy name, Thy nature know.
>
> What though my shrinking flesh complain, And murmur to contend so long?
> I rise superior to my pain, When I am weak, then I am strong

14. This section indebted to Mayes, *Spirituality of Struggle*.

And when my all of strength shall fail, I shall with the God-man prevail.

My strength is gone, my nature dies, I sink beneath Thy weighty hand,
Faint to revive, and fall to rise; I fall, and yet by faith I stand;
I stand and will not let Thee go Till I Thy Name, Thy nature know.

Yield to me now, for I am weak, But confident in self-despair;
Speak to my heart, in blessings speak, Be conquered by my instant prayer;
Speak, or Thou never hence shalt move, And tell me if Thy Name is Love.

'Tis Love! 'tis Love! Thou diedst for me! I hear Thy whisper in my heart;
The morning breaks, the shadows flee, Pure, universal love Thou art;
To me, to all, Thy mercies move; Thy nature and Thy Name is Love.

My prayer hath power with God; the grace Unspeakable I now receive;
Through faith I see Thee face to face, I see Thee face to face, and live!
In vain I have not wept and strove; Thy nature and Thy Name is Love.

I know Thee, Saviour, who Thou art. Jesus, the feeble sinner's friend;
Nor wilt Thou with the night depart. But stay and love me to the end,
Thy mercies never shall remove; Thy nature and Thy Name is Love.

The Sun of Righteousness on me Hath rose with healing in His wings,
Withered my nature's strength; from Thee My soul its life and succour brings;
My help is all laid up above; Thy nature and Thy Name is Love.

Contented now upon my thigh I halt, till life's short journey end;
All helplessness, all weakness I On Thee alone for strength depend;
Nor have I power from Thee to move: Thy nature, and Thy name is Love.

Lame as I am, I take the prey, Hell, earth, and sin, with ease o'ercome;
I leap for joy, pursue my way, And as a bounding hart fly home,
Through all eternity to prove Thy nature and Thy Name is Love.[15]

But what of Wesley's own identity? Who is he, in Christ? In a great hymn, again echoing Jabbok, Wesley delights in his great dignity as a child of God:

15. United Methodist Hymn Book.

Since the Son hath made me free, Let me taste my liberty;
Thee behold with open face, Triumph in Thy saving grace,
Thy great will delight to prove, Glory in Thy perfect love.

Abba, Father! Hear Thy child, Late in Jesus reconciled,
Hear, and all the graces shower, All the joy, and peace, and power,
All my Saviour asks above, All the life and heaven of love.

Lord, I will not let Thee go, Till the blessing Thou bestow;
Hear my advocate divine! Lo! To His my suit I Join;
Joined to His, it cannot fail; Bless me; for I will prevail!

Heavenly Adam, Life divine, Change my nature into Thine!
Move and spread throughout my soul, Actuate and fill the whole!
Be it I no longer now Living in the flesh, but Thou.

Holy Ghost, no more delay! Come, and in Thy temple stay!
Now Thine inward witness bear, Strong, and permanent, and clear;
Spring of Life, Thyself impart, rise eternal in my heart![16]

QUESTIONS FOR REFLECTION

1. Which of the seven elements in the story of Jacob relates most closely to where you are now in your spiritual journey? Why?

2. What threatens our sense of identity today? What affirms us? How can we encourage each other? Read slowly and prayerfully Ps 139:1–18.

3. How can we live out each day our identity as a son or daughter of God? How will this change our attitude to the challenges we face?

4. Which line of Wesley resonates most for you?

5. We learnt that the identity of the Bedouin people of Jabbok/Zarqa is under threat. What other places in the world are you aware of, where identity is undermined by the experience of displacement or environmental damage?

---

16. Methodist Hymn Book.

Monastery of St George Choziba, with Elijah's Cave, above Brook Cherith

3

CHERITH

Living with Paradox

The Lord is my shepherd, I shall not want.
He leads me beside still waters
He restores my soul.
Though I walk through the valley of the shadow of death,
I will fear no evil;
For You are with me;
Your rod and Your staff, they comfort me. (Ps 23:1–4, AV)

Psalm 23 could well be set, say scholars, in the Wadi Qelt, a stunning ravine between Jerusalem and Jericho. It carries the Brook Cherith which enables the flourishing of stunning wildlife and plants along its banks through a desert landscape.[1] David himself knew this valley, for it was along this route that he fled Jerusalem after his son Absalom made himself king (2 Sam 15:23–16:14). Jeremiah was born at Anathoth (Jer 1:1) at the head of the valley, near its spring. Jesus trod this valley on several occasions, as it is the main way to get between Jericho and Jerusalem (Mark 10:46—11:11). Jewish pilgrims would tread this path three times a year for the great Temple festivals, making their climb to Jerusalem, for the approach to the holy city and

---

1. For identification of Wadi Qelt with Cherith see, for example Wilson, *Picturesque Palestine*.

the Mount of Olives (at 2700 feet) from Jericho in the Jordan valley near the Dead Sea, the lowest point on earth, involves an ascent of four thousand feet through the Judean desert. Indeed, the word for pilgrim in Hebrew is *aliyah*, meaning "going up" as in the psalms of ascent: "Jerusalem, built as a city bound firmly together, to which the tribes go up, the tribes of the Lord" (Ps 122). Pilgrims find themselves praying in this spectacular gorge: "I lift up my eyes to the hills— from where will my help come? My help comes from the Lord, who made heaven and earth" (Ps 121).

LAND OF PARADOX

The Judean desert through which the Brook Cherith flows is the archetypal liminal place. It is the space between the City and the River, stretching east from the central highlands towards the fault-line scarp of Jordan's Great Rift Valley. As we consider its story then and now, what comes to the fore is the sense of paradox, even contradiction in the very landscape: it is a land of polarities, even extremes. The Judean desert is a place of dramatic and challenging contrasts: rugged grandeur, raw splendor, untamable beauty, threatening yet inviting, affirming yet disturbing, a place of life and death.

The brook wends its way through a windswept, rocky and rugged wilderness. Mountains tower above sheer limestone cliff walls pock-marked and honeycombed with caves, while chalk hills tower above narrow deeply-incised canyons. The chiseled marl ravines are parchingly dry for much of the year, but in winter, rains from Jerusalem pour through them in torrents forceful enough to move great boulders, which litter the riverbed. Erosion competes with processes of formation: the elements of wind and sun and water split rocks and crumble cliffs, symbolizing the brokenness of humanity, but new shapes and landforms are built up too.

Deep silence is broken only by sounds that ricochet across the canyon. The gurgling water of the stream, with its several waterfalls, echoes between the cliffs. Hungry circling hawks scream overhead, while goats pick their way precariously over the rough terrain, clattering hooves against rocks. By day rock badgers (coneys) scamper and scratch amidst the rocks, while at night the laughing howls of hyenas resound across the valley.

The bleak aridity of the cliffs contrasts with the blossoming of life in the life-giving waters of the Brook Cherith where turquoise-winged kingfisher birds hunt fish: bare rock looks down on lush vegetation of bullrushes, while acacia and juniper trees attempt to cling to the cliffs. Scorching sunlight bounces off white cliffs while cooling patches of shade beckon the weary traveler. Pilgrims get down to the brook: thirst becomes intense in hot summer months but the cooling waters are ready to quench the yearning for refreshment:

> For waters shall break forth in the wilderness, and streams in the desert;
> the burning sand shall become a pool,
> and the thirsty ground springs of water;
> the haunt of jackals shall become a swamp,
>   the grass shall become reeds and rushes. (Isa 35:6, 7)

Paradoxically the Wadi Qelt is a place both of risk and safety. These desert mountains are wild, exposed places, calling forth authenticity and honesty from the soul. They are open places, bespeaking of the vulnerability of the soul. There seems at first no hiding place from the burning sun. Yet the valley walls are peppered with caves where since the fourth century Christian hermits have sheltered and created cells for monastic enclosure. They were vulnerable to raiders (for example, Persians in the seventh century) and before them the valley had witnessed many attacks. Indeed the parable of the good Samaritan is set in this very valley, vividly describing its dangers: "A man was going down from Jerusalem to Jericho, and fell into the hands of robbers, who stripped him, beat him, and went away, leaving him half dead." (Luke 10:30)

The valley's twisting route through the mountains afforded many vantage points of ambush. In AD 70 the 10th Roman Legion marched through this valley to begin their conquest of Jerusalem: remnants of the Roman road are still easily visible today. The Brook Cherith has witnessed highwaymen and peace-loving monks, pilgrims and invaders.

TWO PEOPLES, TWO LIFESTYLES

Settlers and Nomads

The greatest contrast today is between Israeli settlers and Bedouin nomads. Bedouin tribes have lived here for centuries grazing goats and living in their characteristic black tents, occasionally camels nearby. But today they have lost not only their freedom of movement but in places their very ancestral lands.[2] Raja Shedadeh writes: "Perhaps we in Palestine/ Israel should learn

---

2. Some tribes like the Jahalin, were displaced here from ancestral lands in Tel Arad in the Negev in 1948.

from the Bedouin outlook. We haven't yet. Nor are we ever likely to, for one of the tragic consequences of the scramble to possess land following the Israeli occupation was that the Bedouins were pushed out of their traditional grazing grounds. Most of us failed to see that they represent an attractive, alternative way of life and attitude to land that we must all have once shared and from which we still have much to learn."[3]

Since 1967 Israel has built its settlements here. They begin with a hilltop outpost, a few families in caravans, but quickly expand. The settlement of Kfar Adumim was established in 1979 overlooking Wadi Qelt from its southern bank, and today has a population of about five thousand, together with its neighboring settlements Alon and Nofei Prat, founded in 1990 and 1992, respectively. The settlement of Mitzpe Yericho, three thousand strong, is not far away on a neighboring hilltop. As Kfar Adumim grew it confiscated territory from the Palestinian village of Anata (Jeremiah's Anathoth). The tiny settlement Mitzpe Hagit was founded in 1999 on the opposite bank of Wadi Qelt by a family from Alon, and is considered to be a borough of Kfar Adumim. Two miles away lies Ma'ale Adumin, which boasts a staggering 40 thousand residents and has been designated a city.[4] In addition to its red-tile sloping roofs, characteristic of settlements, it has apartment blocks, industrial zones, swimming pool and shopping malls. In the late 1990s, over a thousand Bedouins were displaced from land that was now annexed to form part of the settlement, forced to move when the settlement flooded their encampments with a river of sewage.[5]

The dichotomy between these two types of human habitation are poignantly expressed by Mohammad Korshan, a resident of al-Khan al-Ahmar of the Jahalin Bedouin tribe: "Our lifestyle relies on being able to move around, to live in dispersed tents on large plots of land and raise animals, which we love doing. The Israeli authorities just don't understand our lifestyle."[6] Remnants of the Jahalin live in small numbers in the Wadi Qelt. A people who were characterized by their freedom of lifestyle, moving seasonally with their flocks across the landscape, have now been forcibly and

---

3. Quoted in Murphy, *Between River and Sea*, 325.

4. See Ariel, Allegra and Maggor, *Normalizing Occupation*, 48–63. There are two motivations in settlers: Zionist and religious desires to dwell where patriarchs trod, or economic profit: offered cheap housing by the government, they commute daily into the State of Israel to work. Almost no country recognizes them as legal, since they are on occupied land.

5. Weizman, *Hollow Land*, 21.

6. Abdalla, "Landfill site for Bedouin nomads." See also jahalin.org

repeatedly moved on against their will. Indeed, since the whole area of the Wadi Qelt in this occupied territory has been designated a nature reserve, they are no longer permitted to remain. Raja Shedadeh explains:

> The Bedouin of the Jahalin tribe originally made their home in the Negev, where they lived their nomadic life in tents, raising their goats and occasionally occupying themselves with seasonal agriculture. In 1950 the Israeli army pushed them out and they re-established themselves at the edge of the wilderness, just by Jerusalem, on land that belonged to the Arab village of Abu Dis. They continued living there in their tents, moving eastward in winter to a warmer region, where they stayed until early spring, leaving only after their goats had given birth and the young had grown big enough to move on. But when in 1976 a handful of Israeli families founded the new settlement of Ma'ale Adumim, the Jahalin had to be evicted again... The State was kind enough, after keen media attention, to offer the deposed Bedouins an area near the municipal rubbish dump, from which, years later, they would once again be moved.[7]

In 2014 an eviction order was issued with the intent of removing remaining Bedouin from the Wadi Qelt area to a new town in the Jordan Valley.[8] After being frozen for a time due to international protests, plans to advance with the displacement of Bedouin and the building of 3400 Jewish homes in this part of the West Bank (known as E1) were announced in August 2025.[9]

TWO DIFFERENT PATHS

Elijah at the Brook Cherith

Clinging to the cliffs above the Brook Cherith is the Greek Orthodox monastery of St George Choziba, founded in the fifth century. Here those in residence meet those in transit as the monks graciously welcome pilgrims. The focus of a pilgrim's visit here is the Cave of Elijah, high in the cliff face above the monastery and accessed by a steep staircase. Egeria, the intrepid fourth century Spanish nun, tells us of her visit in the 390s:

---

7. Shedadeh, *Palestinian Walks*, 148, 149.
8. Hass, "Israeli Government Plans."
9. Gritten, "Israel approves controversial West Bank settlement project."

> As we moved along on our journey, we saw a very beautiful valley ahead of us. This was a huge valley that sent a great torrent into the Jordan; and there in that same valley we saw the cell of a certain man, now a brother, by which I mean a monk. So, as I am somewhat curious, I asked what was this valley that a holy person, now a monk, would build a cell for himself there; for I did not think that it would be without some reason. Whereupon, the holy men who were travelling with us and were therefore acquainted with these places told us: "This is the valley of Cherith, where the holy man Elijah the Thesbite, found rest in the days of King Ahab, when there was a famine. A crow, at God's command, brought him food, and he drank water from this torrent which can be seen flowing from this valley into the Jordan, this is the brook Cherith." Once again we gave thanks to God who deigned to show us, who were not deserving, all those things which we yearned to see. We then continued our journey . . .[10]

The Russian abbot Daniel made his visit in 1113, recording:

> The route from Jerusalem to Jordan passes through the Mount of Olives towards the east. This route is very rough and perilous. In the midst of the desolate mountains are found 26 large wells from Jerusalem to Choziba, where Joachim [father of Mary] fasted, to quench our thirst. This place is found in a deep gorge near the route to the left.[11]

Pilgrim Ioannis Fokas from Crete, who travelled to the Holy Land in 1185, leaves us this description:

> There is a great gorge and through it passes a torrent, and on the opposite side is the monastery of Choziba, something which when we are told about can hardly believe . . . And behold, the holes of caves have become the caves of monks and this monastery in the crevices of the rock has its foundations, under the burning sun and with flashes of tongues of fire emitting from the rocks. The water that the monks drink appears to come from a lake [reservoir fed by Cherith], and basking in the midday sun reaches almost a boiling point. In this monastery we saw many blessed men. To this monastery we ventured in a precipitous descent weighted by the heat of the sun.[12]

---

10. Gingras, *Egeria*, 74.
11. Constantinos, *Monastery of Chozeva*, 32.
12. Constantinos, *Monastery of Chozeva*, 33.

What, then, is the significance of this site on the Brook Cherith, in the heart of the Judean wilderness? It preserves an important memory of Elijah, indeed the very beginning of his extraordinary career in the turbulent time of King Ahab in the ninth century BC. The Elijah cycle of stories opens with him speaking God's word of judgement to Ahab, and immediately placing himself in the firing line. God immediately says to him: "Go from here and turn eastward, and hide yourself by the Brook Cherith." Before he goes any further in his prophetic mission, God directs Elijah to a place of contemplation. It is vital that before he commits himself to a life of prophetic speaking and action, Elijah creates a space for silence, listening to God, and stillness. Like the Baptist and Jesus himself in the same desert, Elijah discovers that the prophetic vocation begins in silence.

> And Elijah the Tishbite, of the inhabitants of Gilead, said to Ahab, "As the Lord God of Israel lives, before whom I stand, there shall not be dew nor rain these years, except at my word." Then the word of the Lord came to him, saying, "Get away from here and turn eastward, and hide by the Brook Cherith, which flows into the Jordan. And it will be that you shall drink from the brook, and I have commanded the ravens to feed you there." So he went and did according to the word of the Lord, for he went and stayed by the Brook Cherith, which flows into the Jordan. The ravens brought him bread and meat in the morning, and bread and meat in the evening; and he drank from the brook. And it happened after a while that the brook dried up, because there had been no rain in the land. Then the word of the Lord came to him, saying, "Arise, go to Zarephath, which belongs to Sidon, and dwell there. (1 Kgs 17:1–8, NKJV)

Modeling Paradox

This episode, so formative in Elijah's life, dramatically models and symbolizes the paradox between being settled and being in movement. In the twelfth century Latin Christians came to Mount Carmel (in the north) to live a life in imitation of Elijah's unified life.

They were struck by his zeal and dedication. The first monks interpreted Elijah's "double spirit" asked for by Elisha (2 Kgs 2:9) as representing the coming together of both the active and contemplative life, the "mixed life"—an interplay between contemplative prayer and apostolic action. When in 1210 St Albert, living nearby at Acre, was asked to write for these brothers a Rule to guide their developing lifestyle, he endeavored to strike a fine balance between action and stillness.[13]

Though he was writing for the monks of Mount Carmel, his guidelines can give us too valuable clues for ordering our life aright. Albert's aim was to provide for the brothers of Carmel a life in which all time could be sanctified, "pondering the Lord's law day and night." Within the dynamic between the mystical and prophetic, we need to take another look at the balance in our lives between action and contemplation, between struggle and silence. There is a "a time to speak out and a time to be silent" (Eccl 3:7). As Albert puts it: "Make a balance then, each of you."[14]

In 1370 Felip Ribot, Prior of Catalonian province of Carmelites, explains how this goes back to Elijah at Cherith, in his *Book of the First Monks* (Latin: *Liber de Institutione Primorum Monacharum*):

> The goal of this life is twofold. One part we acquire, with the help of divine grace, through our efforts and virtuous works. This is to offer God a pure heart, free from all stain of actual sin. We do this when we are perfect and in Cherith, that is, hidden in that charity of which the Wise Man says: "Charity covers all sins " [Prov 10:12]. God desired Elijah to advance thus far when He said to him: "Hide yourself by the brook Cherith" [1 Kgs 17:3–4].
>
> The other part of the goal of this life is granted us as the free gift of God: namely, to taste somewhat in the heart and to experience in the soul, not only after death but even in this mortal life, the intensity of the divine presence and the sweetness of the glory of heaven. This is to drink of the torrent of the love of God. God promised it to Elijah in the words: "You shall drink from the brook." It is in view of this double end that the monk ought to give himself to the eremitic and prophetic life.[15]

This highlights a twofold call from God to Elijah at the Cherith: first, "hide yourself by the brook" to find a place of solitude and receive the love of God; second, "drink from the brook" to taste the divine presence. The 1995 *Constitutions of the Carmelite Friars* summarize the way in which these dual strands find expression in the life of Elijah and in Carmelite spirituality today:

---

13. "The Rule of St Albert" translated by Edwards ODC in Obbard, *Land of Carmel.*
14. For Carmelite tradition see Mayes, *Voices from the Mountains.*
15. Copsey, *Way of Life.*

In Elijah we see the solitary prophet who nurtured his thirst for the one and only God, and lived in his presence. He is the contemplative, burning with passionate love for the Absolute who is God, "his word flaring like a torch." He is the mystic who, after a long and wearisome journey, learned to read the new signs of God's presence. He is the prophet who became involved in the lives of the people, and who, by battling against false idols, brought them back to faithfulness to their Covenant with the One God. He is the prophet who was in solidarity with the poor and the forgotten, and who defended those who endured violence and injustice.

From Elijah, Carmelites learn to be people of the desert, with heart undivided, standing before God and entirely dedicated to his service, uncompromising in the choice to serve God's cause, aflame with a passionate love for God. Like Elijah, they believe in God and allow themselves to be led by the Spirit and by the Word that has taken root in their hearts, in order to bear witness to the divine presence in the world, allowing God to be truly God in their lives. Finally, in Elijah they see, not only prophetic wisdom, but also brotherhood lived in community; and with Elijah they learn to be channels of God's tender love for the poor and the humble.[16]

Elijah Lives Out the Two Ways

How did his double call play out in Elijah's subsequent career?

According to the narrative in 1 Kings, three years after the drought began, God asks him to return to Ahab and announce rain (18:2). Elijah is seized by an ambitious plan to show up the deficiency of Jezebel's gods. He challenges Ahab to a showdown, a face-to-face contest with the prophets of Baal on Mount Carmel. After this intense experience, Elijah needs some space: "Elijah went up to the top of Carmel; there he bowed himself down upon the earth and put his face between his knees" (1 Kgs 18:42). After this, Elijah insists on running ahead of Ahab's chariot—over a distance of some thirty miles! On arrival, Elijah is met by a messenger from Jezebel telling him she intends to murder him. He flees for his life—going a considerable distance, over a hundred miles to Beersheva in the south of the country (19:1–3).

There he ventures out into the Negev desert, alone. In the silence Elijah discerns God's response, which is about recovery and pacing himself aright.

16. British Province of Carmelites, *Constitutions*, para 26.

There is a sense, in the account, of a clear set of priorities, an order and progression in God's plan of action for Elijah. First, God answers Elijah's physical needs of exhaustion: he gives him the gift of sleep (19:5). Then, through the agency of the angel, he gives him a hot meal and refreshing drink. Then more sleep is given. This is the first priority—to take efforts to restore the body. Next, God invites Elijah to begin a journey, a pilgrimage to Mount Sinai, Horeb, "the mount of God" (19:7). In calling Elijah to Sinai, God is drawing him back to the wellsprings and fountain of his faith.

So, in the strength of food given him by God, Elijah treks further south to the very place where God first gathered together the people of Israel. What happens there?

> And behold, the Lord passed by, and a great and strong wind rent the mountain, and broke in pieces the rocks before the Lord, but the Lord was not in the wind; and after the wind an earthquake, but the Lord was not in the earthquake; and after the earthquake a fire, but the Lord was not in the fire; and after the fire a still small voice. (19:12,13)

Its clearest meaning, in the context of Elijah's life, is that God is not primarily interested in proving himself in great displays of power, in impressive demonstrations—as Elijah asked him to do on Carmel. The fire, the earthquake, the wind—all speak of stressful ways of working, noisy and disturbing—and God is not to be found in them. Rather he is to be discovered in the still small voice, in the silence. Elijah must make time and space in his life so he will be able to listen and attend to God's voice speaking in the mind, the spirit, the conscience. This voice gets crowded out, drowned by incessant noise and activity. Elijah must learn the secret of stillness—to build into his ministry opportunities to be utterly silent before God, times when God is given a chance to minister to him, times when he can receive from God inner healing and a renewal of his spiritual resources.

But God gives him another safeguard against the threat of stress. "And when Elijah heard it, he wrapped his face in his mantle, and went out and stood at the entrance of the cave" (19:13). Elijah is now leaving his place of hiding, coming out into the open, ready to see horizons again, ready to face the future. Mystic and activist Dorothy Soelle points out:

> [after] the experience of God in the "still, small voice" what happens now? Elijah does not withdraw into an act of worship; he does not make a pilgrimage to some shrine. Nor does he continue to divide things into the categories of sacred and profane, a division

so dear to all religions. Instead, what happens is of significance for the Judeo-Christian tradition: the renewal of his political mission . . . he returns to the world.[17]

She is clear that prayer, if it involves a journey to a world within, must entail the remaking of the self—a re-energizing—so as to enable the return journey to the outer world without delay:

> The goal is to reconcile the two worlds . . . It seems almost impossible to reconcile the two: the magnitude of the inward journey which we need for experience of self, and the way back into the society of a world that can once more be lived in. Inwardness and involvement are not companion attributes in most people, for sensitive people are often not communally inclined, and people who like to be communally involved are sometimes lacking in sensitivity. Prayer and work, labor and contemplation appear to be compartmentalized into two worlds...The critical question with respect to expression of the deepest human experiences, those we regard as "the inward journey," is the question of connection to and with society. . . . Living as Christ lived means the inward journey to the emptying and surrendering of the ego and the return journey to the midst of this world.[18]

It is precisely that we find in the journey within not only an encounter with God but a clarification of our own identity in God, our destiny, and our vocation in the world. The two worlds are one. God gives Elijah a very specific action plan, a clear set of priorities. We read about Elijah's subsequent career in 1 Kings 21 ~ 2 Kings 2. He continues to face big challenges. When Ahab's son sends fifty soldiers to arrest him, they find Elijah "sitting on top of a hill" (2 Kgs 1:9). Has Elijah discovered indeed the crucial importance of making time and space for solitude, for prayer, for God in the midst of a hectic lifestyle? Has he remembered the lesson of the Brook Cherith?

VOICES FROM THE RIVERBANK

In the Byzantine period, the Judean wilderness was flooded with monks seeking seclusion. The title of Derwas Chitty's book, echoing a phrase used by Athanasius in his *Life of Anthony*, sums up the phenomenon: *The Desert*

---

17. Soelle, *Inward Road*, 136.
18. Soelle, *Inward Road*, 55, 56.

a City.[19] At the height of the Byzantine period in the sixth century, there were seventy monasteries in the Judean desert. Today one can visit seven living monasteries and many ruins. In the narrow ravine of the Wadi Qelt we find the very first Judean monastery, founded in 275 by St Chariton (died 350). Today, a sole Russian monk occupies this cave-complex, the silence broken only by the babble of the nearby spring and by birdsong echoing amidst the sheer white cliffs. In the depths of the Wadi Qelt a small community still resides at St George of Choziba. Clearly signposted on the road from Jerusalem to Jericho, not far from Bethany (Lazaria) that clings to the eastern flank of the Mount of Olives, we can find amidst the settlement of Ma'ale Adumin[20] the substantial excavated ruins of the monastery of Euthymius, with their silent but abiding testimony.

EUTHYMIUS THE GREAT

Euthymius (377–473) led the second generation of monks in the Judean mountains above Cherith. We learn about him through *The Life of Euthymius* composed by Cyril of Scythopolis. Born in Melitene in Armenia, after ordination he was placed in charge of the local monasteries around the city but he craved solitude and found this responsibility too onerous, dissipating and distracting, so at the age of 29 (406) he came to the Holy Land as a Christian pilgrim in search of solitude. After venerating the holy places of Jerusalem, he proceeded directly to the desert mountains and "visited the inspired fathers in the desert, studying the virtue and way of life of each one and impressing it upon his own soul."[21] He settled at Chariton's *lavra* (lane linking cells) at Pharan, in the Wadi Qelt. Cyril tells us: "In his love of solitude he stayed in a hermit's cell outside the lavra, possessing absolutely nothing of the goods of this age . . . Freeing himself from every earthly care he had as his one sole aim how to please God through prayer and fasting."[22]

Cyril's account often uses the world *hesychia*—quietude—or *hesychist* (solitary) and tells us of Euthymius' desire to be to be "sundered from all human intercourse and yearning to consort with God in solitude through

---

19. Chitty, *Desert A City*. See also Lane, *Fierce Landscapes*.
20. The name means "Bloody Ascent" referring to the hue of exposed red limestone rocks, tinted by iron oxide.
21. Cyril, *Lives*, 9.
22. Cyril, *Lives*, 9.

prayer."²³ After five years, at the age of 34 (411AD), he moved with his fellow hermit Theoctistus to a cave located on the cliffs of the Wadi Og. Later, more hermits joined them to create a monastery in the form of a *cenobium* (community)—the first in Judean desert. He became famous for healing a son of a Arab leader, and many hermits gathered around him. To further stay in solitude, after ten years in 421 Euthymius relocated with a fellow hermit Domitian to the mountain ruins of Masada, forming the core of a new lavra. After a time living in the cliff-face caves near Tell-Ziph, southeast of Hebron, where he established a further cenobium, he returned to the more remote Monastery of Theoctistus because while he freely offered a ministry of spiritual direction to those who sought him out there, he resolved to safeguard his time alone with God.

Once again, due to his immense popularity, the solitary-seeking hermit moved to a cave west of Theoctistus' monastery on the Adumim hilltop, beside the main road to Jerusalem. In 428 he established here a monastery of hermits based on the model of Chariton's lavra of Pharan. This his successor Martyrius developed into a cenobium. Euthymius' lasting legacy was to establish the pattern for Palestinian monasticism by insisting that those who desired the eremitical (solitary) life must first be trained in the cenobitic community. His voice echoes across the centuries, calling us to vigilance and alertness and humility:

> Brethren, strive for what brought you out here, and do not neglect your own salvation. You must at all times stay sober and awake. As Scripture says, "Keep awake, and pray not to enter into temptation." Above all recognize this: those who renounce this life must not have a wish of their own but in first place acquire humility and obedience.

Euthymius' experience amongst the mountains reveals 3 paradoxes:

1 Solitude and Hospitality

Though Euthymius sought out his mountain-top as a place of retreat from the world, he was ready to welcome seekers and enquirers with their request for guidance: "Give me a word, Father." His life of prayer was situated within the tension of withdrawal and engagement:

---

23. Cyril, *Lives*, 10.

> My child, he who sows with blessings will also reap with blessings. Let us "not neglect to show hospitality, for "thereby (as the Apostle says) some have entertained angels unawares" (Heb 13:2). Be confident that if you and those after you receive with faith and treat worthily all the strangers and brethren who visit you, the Lord will never fail this place from now on till eternity. For God is well-pleased with such an offering . . . [24]

2 Work and Rest

> In addition to keeping watch on the thoughts within, monks, especially young ones, ought to practice bodily labor, remembering the words of the Apostle, "We labor day and night so as not to be a burden on anyone," and "These hands ministered to me and to those with me." While those in the world endure labor and hardship in order to support wives and children from their work, pay the first-fruits to God, do good according to their power and in addition be charged taxes –it is absurd if we are not even to meet the needs of the body from manual labor but to stay idle and immobile, reaping the fruit of the toil of others, especially when the Apostle orders the idle not even to eat.

Cyril adds:

> This was the teaching with which our father Euthymius enlightened the community.[25]

3 Stability and Movement

Although Euthymius found it necessary to travel from time to time, in search of greater solitude, he is an advocate of stability, of staying put:

> Everywhere we need protection by God's help, wherever we are . . . We ought not to admit evil thoughts that insinuate into us a feeling of resentment or loathing towards the place where we are and towards our companions, or implant accidie [listlessness] or suggest moving to other places, but we must at all times be on our guard and oppose the mind to the wiles of the demons for fear that our

---

24. Cyril, *Lives*, 23.
25. Cyril, *Lives*, 13.

rule may be subverted by change of place. For just as a plant that is continuously rebedded cannot bear fruit, so a monk does not bear fruit if he moves from place to place. So if someone resolves to do some good in the place where he is, and is not able to, he should not suppose that he could accomplish it elsewhere. For it is not the place that is in question but the character of the intention.[26]

Such a sentiment can be expressed as "Flourish where you are planted."

An Undistracted Life

Euthymius' Final Testament, given in 473, identifies the overwhelming priority that can shape a settled or peripatetic lifestyle:

> In all things aim at pure love, the source and goal of every good work and the "bread of perfection." Just as it is not done to eat bread without salt, so it is impossible to achieve virtue without love. For each virtue is made secure through love and humility, with the aid of experience, time, and grace. While humility exalts to a height, love prevents falling from this height, "since he who humbles himself will be exalted" and "love never fails." Love is greater than humility, for it was on account of love for us that God the Word humbled himself to become like us. Therefore we ought to confess him from our hearts and address him with hymns and thanksgivings without ceasing, specially we ourselves who are separate from the manifold affairs of this life, not only because of our pledges to him but also by reason of the undistracted life we lead, freed as we are from the confusion of the world. Therefore let us make every effort to offer up to him purity of soul, chastity of body, and pure love . . . [27]

GEORGE OF CHOZIBA (DIED C. 625)

Downstream from Chariton's first monastery, as the Wadi Qelt winds its way towards Jericho, we must visit the monastery of St George, which as we noted preserves the memory of Elijah's sojourn here. Established in about 480 by John of Thebes, it was later dedicated to Saint George of Choziba. He had been born in Cyprus and orphaned at a young age. Coming to the

---

26. Cyril, *Lives*, 26.
27. Cyril, *Lives*, 54, 55.

Judean wilderness, he answered a call to the solitary life: from Saturday evening until Sunday afternoon, George would observe an all-night vigil in the cenobium of his monastery; otherwise he and his fellow monks lived alone in their cells. In 614, when the Persians invaded Palestine and sacked Jerusalem, George refused to quit the monastery: he emerged as a dedicated and courageous abbot.

He loved the Brook Cherith. His biographer Anthony gives us this vignette:

> One day after breakfast I said to the old man, "I'm going to the river to gather caper seeds." And he said to me, "I'll come with you." He was showing his concern for me, for after the Persians came the river had been completely despoiled with wild beasts and unclean spirits. As we were walking along the path between the cells, he said to me "Go down to those caper plants there, child, and gather some, and I'll wait for you here." So I went down and gathered some.
>
> After an hour had passed, he called to me saying, "Come on . . . show me what you have gathered," so I showed him the basket which was about a third full. Groaning aloud he said, "Oh, child, the world is an evil place! Before the Persians came, we were going from our cells to the cenobium for the evening prayers on the [eve of the] Lord's Day when one of the brothers went down to this same caper patch and gathered a full basket, and again in the afternoon the next day when we were returning to our cells, he gathered the same amount." I said to him. "Why is it like this, father?" He said, "At that time holy men were walking about and treading the earth, and the earth was blessed, and everything on it. But now evil-doers and murderers dwell on the earth and thievery and bitterness and adultery and murder are poured out upon it; blood is mixed with blood and the earth is defiled and accused. How can such things on the earth be blessed?"
>
> These were the things he said and taught. They went into my heart so I would write them down just as he said them.[28]

Echoing the vision of those we will meet shortly at the Jordan, George sees the river and environment as sacred. We have to live with another paradox here: to discern the reasons for rivers' despoilation, and to walk ever more reverently upon the earth.

---

28. Vivian, *Journeying Into God*, 101–102.

Cherith

LIVING THE PARADOXES

The challenge of Cherith is that of turning contradictions to be fought into paradoxes to be lived. Indeed, the spiritual life seems to consist of contradictions. We are told about our capacity to bear the divine Spirit—that we are made in the image and likeness of God—but we are all too aware of our mortality, limitations, fragility and failure. There is the constant tension between ideal and reality. With St Paul we cry out: "I do not understand my own actions. For I do not do what I want, but I do the very thing I hate... Who will rescue me..?" (Rom 7:15,24). We are, in Luther's words, *simul justus et peccator*, justified yet sinful.

There are other oppositions we wrestle with. We know we must strive to help build community, but are summoned at times to solitude. I must come to terms with the child and adult in me, masculine and feminine sides to my unique personality. Theologians argue about the interplay between nature and grace, others about determinism and freedom, nature vs. nurture. God is at once immanent and transcendent, close at hand yet seemingly faraway. How can we make sense of these contradictions?

In his teaching, Jesus transforms contradictions into paradoxes. Those who want to save their lives will lose them, and those who lose their lives will save them. The first will be last and the last first. God will exalt the humble and meek and cast down the mighty from their thrones. He makes his sun to rise on rich and poor alike, righteous and unrighteous. The parables declare that weed and wheat are to be permitted to grow together. The beatitudes proclaim the weeping will laugh and the poor possess heaven. The kingdom of God is a topsy-turvy kingdom. It is both "now" and "not yet." Things are inside out, round the wrong way, at least to conventional thinking: this is subversive wisdom that undermines usual patterns of thought. Jesus unites the paradoxes: "in him all things hold together" (Col.1:17).[29]

Maybe Elijah's struggle to discover a balance of prayer and work turns out to be a the key to unlocking knowledge of God:

> This swinging rhythm or oscillation between unlike poles, breathing in and breathing out, speaking and remaining silent, doing and resting, is the basic rhythm of the spiritual life, and it is only within the rhythm that we can know God, experience him, think and talk about him. If we abandon ourselves to this rhythm, let

---

29. See de Waal, *Living with Contradiction*.

ourselves be carried by it, it will gradually kindle with us the spark of Divine Knowledge.[30]

The Invitation of the Brook Cherith

In our sojourn in the Wadi Qelt we have noticed how a single landscape embraces vastly contrasting lifestyles. This overwhelming message of the Brook Cherith as it courses through the Wadi Qelt speaks both to personal and political realities today.

Elijah at the Brook Cherith invites us to balance the twin demands of action and contemplation within a single lifestyle of ministry and prayer. His own experience reveals how stillness and settlement can co-exist with movement and travel: residence and transience greet each other. George balances hermitage and cenobium, while Euthymius' life vacillates between stability and peripatetic as he wrestles with the interplay between solitude and hospitality, work and rest, stability and movement.

In this spirit, Bedouin nomads and Israeli settlers can co-exist, too, perhaps, beside and above the Brook Cherith. There is space enough for hilltop settlements and hillside camps. We can all learn from the example of one of the monks—he remains anonymous—whom John Moschos heard about in 600 AD living above the brook:

> When he went into the wilderness and settled at the Cells of Choziba this elder was greatly considerate of his neighbors. He would travel the road from the holy Jordan to the Holy City of Jerusalem carrying bread and water. And if he saw a person overcome by fatigue, he would shoulder that person's pack and carry it all the way to the holy Mount of Olives. He would do the same on the return journey if he found others, carrying their packs as far as Jericho. You would see this elder, sometimes sweating under a great load, sometimes carrying a youngster on his shoulders. There was even an occasion when he carried two of them at the same time. Sometimes he would sit down and repair the footwear of men and women if this was needed, for he carried with him what was needed for that task. To some he gave a drink of the water that he carried with him and to others he offered bread. If he found anyone naked, he would give him the very garment he wore. You saw him working all the day long.[31]

---

30. Smith, *Way of Paradox*, 26.
31. Moschos, *Spiritual Meadow*, 16.

The first line of the account tells us he was "settled"—and finding time, somehow, to pray alone and to worship with his brothers. The account ends: "You saw him working all the day long." A rare combination—but evidently possible—the paradox of combining stillness and considerable movement! No doubt the movement was fueled and energized by the prayer!

QUESTIONS FOR REFLECTION

1. In what ways do the calls to stillness and movement, silence and talking, play out in your life? How do you live in what Soelle calls "the two worlds" of inward journey and outward engagement?
2. In what ways can you identify with Elijah's experience?
3. How can the concept of "living the paradox" help make sense of conflicting demands?
4. What strikes you most from the examples of Euthymius and George?
5. The presence of Israeli settlers on occupied land and their building of substantial settlements on confiscated property is a matter of deep controversy. Where do you stand on the issue? In what ways might the co-existence of settlers and Bedouin be reconcilable? How can these "two worlds" beside and above Cherith meet?

Israeli, Palestinian, and Jordanian youth call for Jordan River rehabilitation

4

JORDAN

Renewing Creation

I remember thee from the land of the Jordan.
Deep calleth unto deep at the noise of thy waterfalls:
All thy waves and thy billows are gone over me.
Yet God will command his lovingkindness in the day-time;
And in the night his song shall be with me,
Even a prayer unto the God of my life. (Ps 42:6–8 ASV)

THE RIVER JORDAN GETS its name from the Hebrew *Yarden*, meaning "to descend." It begins its life in the gushing springs of Banias, Dan and Hatsbani—melting snows sink deep into Mount Hermon, forming subterranean water ways until they emerge at its foothills. It cascades through the verdant Galilean hills, eroding its way to the Sea of Galilee. A severe limit has been enforced allowing precious water to flow from the reservoir of the Sea of Galilee down to the Dead Sea 1200 feet below sea level, so south of the lake the Jordan becomes more of a stream, flowing in a hidden channel cut into the valley floor, bounded to east and west by the precipitous limestone escarpment cliffs of the great African-Syrian rift. To the east rise the mountains of Gilead and Moab, while on the west bank the mountains of the Judean desert make their presence felt as one follows the flow southwards. An area closely associated both with John the Baptist and Elijah is known as the "Pride of Jordan"—a jungle of willows and papyrus reeds cloaks the banks of the river.

We have many testimonies to the speed of the fast flowing waters of the Jordan, even in its lower reaches. Pilgrim accounts tell us how dynamic was the river. In 1103 Saewulf tells us: "Now the river Jordan, flowing from its spring with a very rapid course, falls into the Sea of Galilee on one side, and passing out of it on the opposite side, by the violence of its current, makes itself a bed through which it runs a distance of eight days' journey, and then falls into the Dead Sea."[1]

Writing in 1894 George Adam Smith observed: "The swiftness is rendered more dangerous by the muddy bed and curious zigzag current which will easily sweep a man from the side into the center of the stream . . . It tumbles and rushes south through a stretch of 137 miles till it sweeps, with a strong and level current, into the Dead Sea . . . the extraordinary valley is chiseled on a running slope down to the depths of the earth."[2]

The Degradation of the Jordan

Today the waters of the lower Jordan are murky and sluggish. Since 1948 both Israel and the state of Jordan have diverted a staggering 96% of the Jordan's water after its outflow from the Sea of Galilee—for irrigation purposes. This has reduced a once mighty fast-flowing river coursing down the rift valley to little more than a muddy trickle. In addition, pollution has become a major problem as effluents have been allowed to enter the river system. Moreover for a long section of the river has been a heavily mined military area since 1967—a no-go area. (Prior to this, from 1964–1967, a series of confrontations between Israel and its Arab neighbors, known as the "War over Water" or the "Battle over Water," took place over control of water sources in the Jordan River drainage basin).

Today, the River has become an ecological emergency. Too polluted for baptisms, it is dangerously contaminated, and in 2010 pilgrims were advised not to enter the water at all at the historic baptismal site of Qasar al-Yahud.[3] Meanwhile the level of the Dead Sea has shrunk dramatically in recent years due to the decreased flow from the Jordan. Once sacred waters have become desecrated.

1. Wright, *Early Travels*, 47.
2. Smith, *Historical Geography*, 486.
3. Sherwood, "Pollution Fears at River Jordan Pilgrimage Spot."

JORDAN

JORDAN IN BIBLE—PLACE OF NEW BEGINNINGS

In the Scriptures the Jordan has been a place of new beginnings. With great joy Joshua led the Israelites across the river as the conclusion of their long Exodus journey. It marked their point of entry into the Promised Land:

> When the people set out from their tents to cross over the Jordan, the priests bearing the ark of the covenant were in front of the people. Now the Jordan overflows all its banks throughout the time of harvest. So when those who bore the ark had come to the Jordan, and the feet of the priests bearing the ark were dipped in the edge of the water, the waters flowing from above stood still, rising up in a single heap far off at Adam, the city that is beside Zarethan, while those flowing towards the sea of the Arabah, the Dead Sea, were wholly cut off. Then the people crossed over opposite Jericho. While all Israel were crossing over on dry ground, the priests who bore the ark of the covenant of the Lord stood on dry ground in the middle of the Jordan, until the entire nation finished crossing over the Jordan. (Josh 3:14–17)

It was a new beginning too for the pagan military commander Naaman (9th cent. BC) who had suffered for years with leprosy:

> Naaman came with his horses and chariots, and halted at the entrance of Elisha's house. Elisha sent a messenger to him, saying, "Go, wash in the Jordan seven times, and your flesh shall be restored and you shall be clean." But Naaman became angry and went away, saying . . . "Are not Abana and Pharpar, the rivers of Damascus, better than all the waters of Israel? Could I not wash in them, and be clean?" . . . He went down and immersed himself seven times in the Jordan, according to the word of the man of God; his flesh was restored like the flesh of a young boy, and he was clean. Then he returned to the man of God, he and all his company; he came and stood before him and said, "Now I know that there is no God in all the earth except in Israel." (2 Kgs 5:9–12,14–15)

For Christians, the greatest event in the Jordan is of course the baptism of Jesus:

> In those days Jesus came from Nazareth of Galilee and was baptized by John in the Jordan. And just as he was coming up out of the water, he saw the heavens torn apart and the Spirit descending like a dove upon him. And a voice came from the heavens, "You are my Son, the Beloved; with you I am well pleased." (Mark 1:9–11)

Mark, characteristically, expresses the mystery in a few well-chosen words. But what is the significance of Jesus' baptism? In particular, does it have any ecological significance that might speak to the present situation of conflict and degradation at the Jordan? I have written elsewhere about the liminal character of the Jordan—its role as a threshold which Jesus crosses as he wades in deep rough water from the east (John 1:28) to the west (Mark 1:12), signifying leaving one world represented in the phrase "Nazareth of Galilee" and entering another.[4] In *Holy Land? Challenging Questions from the Biblical Landscape* I explored how the issue of identity is central to the event, not only for Jesus himself but for all of us.[5] But is there anything to be discovered about its environmental importance?

THE RENEWAL OF ALL CREATION

For the Orthodox tradition one emphasis, rarely considered in the West, is paramount: in the coming of Jesus to the Jordan we see the entry of the divine Creator Word, made flesh (John 1:18), into the very midst of creation, as the deep and powerful currents of the Jordan swirl around him. At the self-same moment as the naked body of the incarnate creator Word is submerged, enveloped, inundated by the waters, the divine Spirit descends in an echo from Genesis 1:2

> The earth was complete chaos, and darkness covered the face of the deep, while a wind from God swept over the face of the waters. (NRSV)

> Earth was a soup of nothingness, a bottomless emptiness, an inky blackness. God's Spirit brooded like a bird above the watery abyss. (Message)

> The earth was formless and void, a waste and emptiness, and darkness was upon the face of the deep primeval ocean that covered the unformed earth. The Spirit of God was moving, hovering, brooding over the face of the waters. (AMP)

The early Church fathers noted its significance. Cyril of Alexandria (376–444), in his commentary on Matthew 3 declares: "Christ was not baptized as one repenting but as one cleansing sins and sanctifying the waters" (Fragment 29, *Stromateis*.) Maximus of Turin (380–420) puts it: "Christ is

---

4. Mayes, *Beyond the Edge*.
5. Mayes, *Holy Land?*

baptized, not to be made holy by the water, but to make the water holy, and by his cleansing to purify the waters which he touched. For the consecration of Christ involves a more significant consecration of the water. For when the Savior is washed all water is made clean, purified at its source for the dispensing of baptismal grace to the people of future ages."[6]

Professor Ioannes Fountoulis celebrates the sacrality of the River:

> First, as the beginning and the head of the new people, Christ is baptized and sanctifies the created waters to create through them the new world, the New Creation, new people, faithful Christbearers and Godbearers. In the celebration of the Theophany, after the blessing of the water and the communion and the sprinkling of believers, the catechumens were baptized. It was the feast of "the Lights." The "illumination"—the baptism of Christ and Christians.[7]

Christ by His baptism sanctifies this water and makes it the means, not only of our healing by partaking of it, but of the renewal of the creation. All creation is sanctified by means of Christ's Baptism, beginning with that most basic element of creation—water. It was the mystical waters that were separated to form the heavens and the earth. So, with the sanctification of water, all creation becomes good, pure again; it becomes what it first was, it returns to its first beauty. It takes on a "spiritual" attribute, that is, it is renewed as a means of communicating God's grace. Elizabeth Scalia puts it:

> With Christ's baptism, God no longer moved upon the face of the water, he was immersed within it — and not thoughtlessly, as a child playing in a river, but God-mindfully; with an intention to save. The whole body of Christ Jesus, intentionally submerged by John (by Christ's command), enhanced and perhaps exceeded creation; rather than God's Spirit moving upon the face of things, God Incarnate — *Emmanuel* — sanctified the water with his very flesh. And the water flowed, and it fed streams and animals and plants, and it rose, and it fell and it renewed the face of the earth in the most mystical of ways, because it was now, and forever more, *holy* water — literally touched by God, with an intention full of love and mercy. God particles, multiplied into infinity, and all around us, contained in all that grows and flows.[8]

---

6. Maximus of Turin, "Sermon for the Feast of the Epiphany."
7. Fountoulis, "Theophany."
8. Scalia, "Christ is baptized."

The Blessing of the Waters

"Christ has shone forth in the Jordan to sanctify the waters." The Orthodox celebration of the Baptism of Christ in the feast of the Theophany is no mere recalling of an historical event but rather a celebration of the present reality. The celebration reaches its climax with the ceremony of the Blessing of the Waters, taking place at a local river or around a font or bowl of water placed in the center of the church building. Surrounded by candles and flowers, this water stands for the beautiful world of God's original creation and ultimate glorification by Christ in the Kingdom of God, and this hymn is sung:

> Let us the faithful praise the greatness of God's plan for us.
> For He Who alone is pure and undefiled
> becomes a man because of our transgressions.
> He is cleansed with our cleansing in the Jordan,
> sanctifying both us and the waters,
> and crushing the heads of the dragons in the water.
> Therefore, let us draw water in gladness,
> for upon those who draw in faith
> the grace of the Spirit is invisibly bestowed by Christ God,
> the Savior of our souls.[9]

This hymn expresses the thought-world of the Ancient Near East, where the waters of sea or river were feared as the abode of chaos. The waters are brimming with demons and monsters. We even know their names! Here lurks Leviathan and Rahab (Ps 74:13–14). For the first readers of the Gospels, the very mention of the sea evokes the primordial chaos of Genesis 1, while their hopes for the End Time are expressed in the final defeat of the beast in the sea, as in Daniel and Revelation: indeed, at the End, "there is no more sea"—no more chaos (Rev 21:1). This is all very much part of the biblical mindset which can be traced across the Ancient Middle East: the Babylonian Epic of Gilgamesh conceives the waters as a place of danger and terror, while the Ugarit texts narrate how Baal battles with the sea-god Yam. This belief finds another echo:

> "O Prophet," the Lord now says to John,
> "come and baptize Me, thy Creator,
> for I cleanse and enlighten all with grace!
> Touch My divine head and do not hesitate!
> O Prophet, let it be so now;

---

9. Orthodox Church in America.

> for I have come to fulfill all righteousness!
> Make haste; for I hasten to destroy the Enemy,
> the prince of darkness, hidden in the waters,
> that I might deliver the world from his snares,
> and in My love grant eternal life!"

As the priest holds a wooden Cross in his hands, to be cast upon the face of the waters, this great hymn by Sophronios, Patriarch of Jerusalem is sung:

> The voice of the Lord is upon the waters crying:
> "Come, one and all,
> receive the Spirit of wisdom,
> the Spirit of understanding,
> the Spirit of the fear of God,
> from Christ Who now has shone forth!"
>
> Today the nature of the waters is sanctified:
> The Jordan is parted in two.
> It holds back the flow of its waters,
> as it beholds the washing of the Master.
>
> Today Thou hast appeared to the universe,
> Thy Light, O Lord, has shone on us, who with understanding praise Thee:
> Thou hast come and revealed Thyself, O Light Unapproachable![10]

This celebration, uniquely, draws us to a key meaning hidden in the event of the baptism of Christ in the Jordan. The entry of the Word into the center of creation resanctifies, reconsecrates creation, and declares the natural world sacred, to be treated with reverence, because it is infused with the Divine—indeed it is God-bearing, God-revealing, an Epiphany, Theophany, a veritable sacrament. Alexander Schmemann sums it up in the title of his great book *The World as Sacrament*:

> What is important for us is that the baptismal water represents the matter of the cosmos, the world as life of humanity. Its blessing acquires thus a cosmic and redemptive significance. God created the world and blessed it and gave it to humanity as food and life, as a means of communion with him. The blessing of the water signifies the return or redemption of matter to this initial and essential meaning. By accepting the baptism of John, Christ sanctified the water—made it the water of purification and reconciliation with God. It was then, as Christ was coming out of the water, that the Epiphany—the new and redemptive manifestation of God—took place, and the Spirit of God, who at the beginning of creation

---

10. Orthodox Church in America.

"moved upon the face of the waters," made water—that is, the world—again into what he made them at the beginning.... Once more the world is proclaimed to be what Christ revealed and made it to be—the gift of God to humanity, the means of humanity's communion with God . . . Faith in Christ that leads a person to baptism today is precisely the certitude that Christ is the only true "content" —meaning, being and end—of all that exists, the fulness of him who fills all things. In faith the whole world becomes the sacrament of his presence, the means of life in him. And water, the image and presence of the world, is truly the image and presence of Christ.[11]

As the Ecumenical Patriarch has said more recently:

> The Lord suffuses all of creation with His Divine presence in one continuous legato from the substance of the atoms to the Mind of God. Let us renew the harmony between heaven and earth, and transfigure every detail, every particle of life. Let us love one another, and lovingly learn from one another, for the edification of God's people, for the sanctification of God's creation, and for the glorification of God's most holy Name.[12]

VOICES FROM THE RIVERBANK

Returning to Paradise

"And the Spirit immediately drove him out into the wilderness. He was in the wilderness for forty days, tempted by Satan; and he was with the wild beasts; and the angels waited on him" (Mark 1:12,13). Straight after his baptism Jesus goes to live in closest proximity to wildlife. The wild beasts of the desert near the Jordan include lions, hyenas and jackals. When the Desert Fathers and Mothers begin to seek a life of prayer in this wilderness, they understand their quest in terms of a return to Paradise—living so close to nature, even in such terrain, they feel as if they have recovered something of Eden before it was lost by Adam's fall, for here they can find unbroken communion with God amidst raw nature, trees, plants and animals. Images such as Elijah being fed by ravens by the Brook Cherith reinforced this desire to live in communion with the natural world. Elsewhere (Scetis) Cassian calls his desert environment "a true paradise of perfection."[13]

---

11. Schmemann, *World as Sacrament*, 88–90.
12. Ecumenical Patriarch Bartholomew, "Presentation to Metropolitan Nikitas."
13. Cassian, *Conferences*, 1.1

For them the land is indeed sanctified and sacred. Their wisdom and experiences, collected up as *The Sayings of the Desert Fathers* is simply called by eastern Christians *The Paradise* or *The Monks' Garden*. Though sometimes depicted as other-worldly they in fact reveal both a spiritual and practical appreciation of the natural world and of the environment in which their lives are set.

Living with Lions

John Moschos tells us the story of **Gerasimos** and the lion.[14] Saint Gerasimos (d. 475) established a monastery near the River Jordan—it is still very active to this day and can be visited, being located only a mile from the Baptismal site. One day Saint Gerasimos met close to the monastery a lion who was in great pain due to a large splinter embedded in his paw. Saint Gerasimos, full of love for the entire nature and moved by the Holy Spirit, did not hesitate a second. He put all human fear away and he removed the splinter and cleansed the lion's wound. Feeling great gratitude the lion followed him back to the monastery and became his devoted pet. All the monks were amazed at the animal's conversion to a peaceful pet, living only on bread and vegetables. The lion was given the task of guarding the monastery's donkey.

However, one day the donkey was stolen while the lion was sleeping. The monks thought that the lion had eaten the donkey and as punishment they gave the lion the job of the donkey: to carry water from the Jordan river to the monastery. Several months later the thief was passing by the Jordan with the stolen donkey and three camels. The lion recognized the donkey and chased the thief away, bringing the donkey back to the monastery—along with the thief's camels. The monks realized their mistake and understood that the lion was fully devoted to Gerasimos and their monastery. After five years, when Gerasimos died, the lion lay down on his grave and died too. The icon of Gerasimos always depicts him with the lion at his side.

John the Hesychast (454–558) was to live in solitude in the Judean wilderness near the Jordan for 76 years, earning the name "John the Silent." At a time when attacks on monasteries and monks by Saracens made this life

---

14. Moschos, *Spiritual Meadow*, 86.

very dangerous, he was being persuaded to abandon his remote cave at Rouba near the Dead Sea but

> He made the Most High his refuge, and remained undaunted . . . Out of a wish to reassure John, who had felt some slight fear, God sent, as a visible protector, an enormous and terrifying lion to protect him day and night from the plots of the wicked barbarians. The first night he saw the lion lying beside him he naturally felt some slight fear, as he himself related to me; but when he saw that the lion followed him day and night as his inseparable companion and warded off the barbarians, he offered up hymns of thanksgiving to God for "not releasing the staff of sinners onto the lot of the righteous." (Ps 125:3)[15]

Abba Alexander of the lavra of Calamon by the Jordan tells us about an unexpected visitor:

> One day when I was with Abba Paul the Greek at his cave, somebody came and knocked at the door. The elder went out and opened to him. Then he took out and set before him bread and soaked peas, which he wolfed down. I thought it must be some stranger; I looked a through the window and saw that it was a lion. I said to the elder: "Good elder, why do you feed that animal? Explain to me." He said, "I have required of it that it neither harm man nor beast; and I have told it to come here each day and I will give it its food. It has come twice a day now for seven months—and I feed it."[16]

Like St Francis who in a later century will feed the fearsome wolf of Gubbio, Abba Paul feeds the lion—hoping that it will remain vegetarian and not harm anybody! John Moschos gives us this brief vignette:

> There was another elder at that place [near the Jordan] called Sapsas whose virtue was so great that he would welcome the lions which came into his cave and feed them at his lap, so full of divine grace was this man.[17]

We will meet **Saba**, perhaps the most significant monk of the Judean desert near the Jordan, in the next chapter. For the moment, we can note two significant stories about him from the narratives of Cyril of Scythopolis. For a season, Saba needed to withdraw from the Kidron valley:

15. Cyril, *Lives*, 231.
16. Moschos, *Spiritual Meadow*, 134
17. Moschos, *Spiritual Meadow*, 5.

> He withdrew to the region of Scythopolis [further up in the Jordan valley]; he settled in a desert spot by the river called Gadaron, and stayed there for a short time in a cave where an enormous lion was wont to withdraw. Around midnight this lion returned and found the blessed one sleeping. Taking hold of his patchwork habit with its mouth, it began to pull at him, striving to remove him from the cave. When he got up and began the night psalmody, the lion went out and waited outside the cave; when the old man had completed the office and lay down in the place where the lion was wont to lie down, it came in again and, taking hold of his patchwork habit, began to pull at him, trying to remove him from the cave. So, with the lion pressing him to leave the cave, the old man said to him in confidence of spirit, "The cave is spacious enough to provide plentiful lodging for the two of us, for we both have one Creator. As for you, if you want, stay here!"[18]

As in the tale of Gerasimos, donkeys have their role too in Saba's experience. Since they were in straits because of the lack of water, Saba prayed one night for refreshment:

> ... while he was making this prayer in the little oratory, he heard the hoof-beat of a wild ass in the gorge below. Peering down (it was full moon), he saw a wild ass digging deep into the earth with its hooves; when it had dug a large hole, he saw it lowering its mouth into the hole and drinking. Reflecting that rather God was making a visitation and bringing forth water for his servants, he immediately climbed down and, digging the place, found flowing water. And lo, in the middle of this lavra this water exists today, providing much relief to the fathers....[19]

Living with Nature

The desert fathers and mothers who lived near the Jordan in the fourth to seventh centuries have much to teach us about living simply. They had an appreciation of the beauty of the natural world. For example, as we noted in the last chapter, the need for solitude moved individual monks to depart to the far reaches of the wilderness for a season. Euthymius, in 411, initiated the practice of leaving the monastic community and traveling into the inner desert in Palestine. Following the example of Christ, he would

---

18. Cyril, *Lives*, 127, 128.
19. Cyril, *Lives*, 110.

depart on the Feast of Christ's Baptism (the 14th of January) and return for Palm Sunday. Until his death at age 90, he went annually with his friends, sometimes including Saba and Gerasimos, subsisting on herbs and what water they could find, to such sites as Masada and the wild gorges above the Dead Sea. On their return, they would either go back to the monasteries, or "armed with those lovely little flowers of many colors that show themselves in the spring in the most barren places of the wilderness" travel to Olivet. Perhaps they scattered the flowers in the annual Palm Sunday procession down the Mount of Olives?[20]

Other vignettes give us clues about their simple lifestyle in which they walked reverently upon the earth. They cultivated little gardens, growing vegetables and fruit trees like carob and even fig:

> The spot where the holy elder was enclosed has to the west a very high cliff, which the roof of the cell rests against. The rock of the cliff is so dry and moistureless that it does not cause the least damp to the cell. One day, taking the seed of a fig, the holy elder Saba said to his disciples Theodore and John, "Listen to me my children. If God in his mercy gives grace to this seed and power to this rock to bear fruit, know that he bestows on me as a gift the kingdom of heaven." Saying this he pressed the fig seed against the smooth rock. The same God who ordered the rod of Aaron, despite its dryness, to grow and flower ordered this smooth and utterly dry rock to bring forth . . . The shoot, gradually growing in height and reaching the roof, which it even covered over, proceeded with the passing of time to produce three figs. Taking and kissing these with tears, the elder tasted them, rendering thanks to God for this assurance—and giving a little of them to his disciples . . .

Cyril adds his own testimony about a partnership between human and creation:

> I, on coming to him and seeing the awesome sight of the shoot exclaimed in astonishment, "O the depths of the riches and wisdom and knowledge of God, how unsearchable are his judgements and inscrutable his ways!" Rarely do figs or any tree grow here, because of the great heat and dryness of the lavra. If anyone adduces the trees of the little cenobium of the lavra that grow along the road, he should know that these were the work of the blessed Saba, who found depth of soil and a supply of rainwater from the gorge, and

---

20. Chitty, *Desert A City*, 96.

of the fathers of the same little cenobium, who to this day water
them throughout the winter with water from the gorge.[21]

The monks living near the Jordan were mainly self-sufficient, raising a little income from working with local natural materials and weaving mats, baskets and rope from palm leaves.

Though the desert fathers come over sometimes as a bit hard-edged in their ascetic disciplines, not suffering fools gladly, such stories also reveal a tenderness towards creation and deepest respect. They reveal in their lifestyles a belief in the sanctification of the earth celebrated at the Jordan and tread lightly on the earth. They were inspired by the prophetic words of Isaiah:

> The wolf shall live with the lamb,
> > the leopard shall lie down with the kid,
> the calf and the lion and the fatling together,
> > and a little child shall lead them.
> The cow and the bear shall graze,
> > their young shall lie down together;
> > and the lion shall eat straw like the ox.
> The nursing child shall play over the hole of the asp,
> > and the weaned child shall put its hand on the adder's den.
> They will not hurt or destroy
> > on all my holy mountain;
> for the earth will be full of the knowledge of the Lord
> > as the waters cover the sea. (Isa 11:8–9)
>
> For the Lord will comfort Zion; he will comfort all her waste places, and will make her wilderness like Eden, her desert like the garden of the Lord; joy and gladness will be found in her, thanksgiving and the voice of song. (Isa 51:3)

For these early Christian dwellers on the banks of the Jordan and its environs, the natural world was dynamic. They lived in a universe alive and brimming with the Divine. They enjoyed a conscious relationship with the earth, living in communion with their terrain where they naturally expected to discover and welcome signs of God's presence and provision. The sayings and tales that have come down to us reveal a tender, reverential attitude to the natural world that spills over into a spirit of generosity and respect of the Other.

---

21. Cyril, *Lives*, 239–240.

RENEWING THE JORDAN

Some hopeful signs are emerging of a new resolve to respond to the degradation of the Jordan River. The *Times of Israel* reports a breakthrough in the deadlock that had led to inaction:

> The Israeli and Jordanian governments signed at the UN COP27 a declaration of intent on 27 November 2022 to partner in the ecological restoration and sustainable development of the Jordan River.
>
> According to the Environmental Protection Ministry, restoration of the Jordan River is a major goal for both countries due to its great ecological value, its rich historical and religious heritage, and its importance as a major tourist site.
>
> The agreement gives practical expression to Annex 4 of the 1994 Israel-Jordanian Peace Treaty, which contains clauses regarding environmental cooperation in the Jordan River. These include the ecological restoration of the waterway, protection of water resources from pollution, control of agricultural pollution and waste, pest control, the creation of nature reserves and protected areas, and tourism and historical heritage.
>
> Both countries pledged to treat pollution in their respective territories, partly by building wastewater treatment facilities and connecting towns along the river to advanced sewage infrastructure. They will also improve the quality of the water that flows into what has become, in many parts, little more than a polluted, trickling stream.
>
> The two sides also agreed to promote sustainable agriculture, with special emphasis on regulating agricultural runoff and reducing the use of chemical pesticides. The two countries also committed to examining the creation of a regional research center and academic cooperation aimed at restoring the streams that run into the Jordan River.
>
> In July 2022, the Israeli government approved an ambitious plan to clean up a substantial stretch of the Jordan River, restore its once abundant nature, and develop tourism along its banks.[22]

Minister of Environmental Protection Tamar Zandberg declared: "Cleaning up the pollutants and hazards, restoring water flow and strengthening the natural ecosystems will help us prepare and adapt to the climate crisis." EcoPeace Middle East, a cross-border environmental group that has promoted Israeli-Jordanian-Palestinian cooperation on water issues, said the

---

22. Surkes, "Agreement to clean up Jordan River."

agreement to rehabilitate the Jordan River was "a critical climate adaptation measure that can help bring back 50% of the biodiversity lost because of decades of pollution and freshwater diversion."[23]

The November 2022 agreement has the status of a "declaration of intent." We trust that practical steps will be taken, in the River that foreshadows the death and resurrection of Christ, to bring renewal and regeneration to its sacred waters. We might all heed the counsel of Zossima:

> Brothers, have no fear of men's sin. Love a man even in his sin, for that is the semblance of Divine Love and is the highest love on earth. Love all God's creation, the whole and every grain of sand in it. Love every leaf, every ray of God's light. Love the animals, love the plants, love everything. If you love everything, you will perceive the divine mystery in things. Once you perceive it, you will begin to comprehend it better every day. And you will come at last to love the whole world with an all-embracing love.[24]

QUESTIONS FOR REFLECTION

1. The word for "pollution" in the Hebrew Scriptures, used over 200 times, carries the meaning of desecrating something that is holy, defiling the sacred. How can this sense inform our concerns about the pollution of rivers today?
2. In what ways can you live more alertly with a sense of "sacred earth"—the sanctification of the natural world?
3. Where do you glimpse the Divine in creation? What is most surprising for you about this?
4. What issues of pollution do you find in your own setting? Is there anything you can do about it?
5. What strikes you most from the Voices from the Riverbank?

---

23. Debre, "Israel and Jordan." See also Global Freshwater Initiative, "Jordan River Project." For update, see EcoPeace, "Rehabilitation in Jordan Valley."
24. Dostoyevsky, *Brothers Karamazov*, Ch. III.

Polluted Kidron stream flowing past Mar Saba monastery in the Judaean desert

5

KIDRON

Making Life-changing Decisions

*Multitudes, multitudes,
in the valley of decision! (Joel 3:14)*

THE KIDRON VALLEY BEGINS just north east of the Old City of Jerusalem in the Wadi El Joz, Valley of the Walnuts. Its route follows the foot of the Mount of Olives and the Garden of Gethsemane to the east and the wall of the old city, with its Golden Gates and Temple Mount/ Noble Sanctuary to the west: as dawn rises above the Mount of Olives the city walls above the Kidron begin to glow. At the south eastern corner of the city, below Mount Zion/ the Ophel Ridge it joins with the Hinnom and Tyropean Valleys as it passes through the Arab village of Silwan (Siloam), and thence weaves its way as a ravine through the mountains of the Judean Desert, descending 4,000 feet along its twenty mile course through Occupied Territory until it reaches the Dead Sea. Towering cliffs frame its passage through the Judean wilderness. In the chasm where Mar Saba monastery has stood since the fourth century, the roar of its flow ricochets across the valley walls. . . . ..

But in recent years the flow of the river beside the Old City was diverted underground because it became a major sewer: emerging above ground, it has caused severe environmental damage in the ravine and in the Dead Sea. While one million cubic meters of pure water flowed into it from the sacred Gihon Spring, 20 million cubic meters of untreated sewage entered it from Jerusalem, joined by five million cubic meters from Bethlehem and other Palestinian towns and villages. In the valley known as the Valley of Decision this has afforded an appalling example of indecision and procrastination by Israeli and Palestinian authorities. It has been called "The most breath-taking example of joint neglect in the Middle East."[1] Jones' *Dictionary of Old Testament Proper Names* translates Kidron as "very black, full of darkness." Kidron in Hebrew can mean darkness, turbulence, great agitation and great evil.

But recently there has been a new and hopeful light shining on the valley: after years of wrangling a breakthrough and a courageous joint decision-making is restoring the "environmental dignity" of the river. In a rare collaboration with the Palestinian Authority, Jerusalem's municipal water and waste water corporation Hagihon is leading the Kidron stream rehabilitation project in which the sewage flow to the stream will be stopped and diverted to a new collection line. Thirty seven kilometers of sewage pipes need to be laid, with a treatment facility built in the heart of the Judean Desert to absorb sewage flowing in the valley. Avi Balashnikov, chairman of the Gihon Corporation and the Jerusalem Sewage and Wastewater Treatment Plants Company declares: "The rehabilitation of the Kidron Valley will regulate the problem of wastewater discharge in the Kidron Basin and serve all the communities along the valley. We will restore to the Kidron Valley the majesty and splendor of the environmental, heritage, tourism and historical splendor."[2] A creative decision indeed!

THE VALLEY OF DECISION

> For the day of the Lord is near
> in the valley of decision. (Joel 3:14)

Joel refers in the first instance to the divine decision-making on the Day of Judgement[3], but his words resonate across the centuries to characterize human action in this valley. Critical and momentous choices have been made in this very valley, that have had far-reaching implications...

---

1. Lupin, "Kidron Valley."

2. Jerusalem Post, "NIS One billion Kidron Valley Rehabilitation Project Progresses." Equivalent to 300 million dollars or 240 million pounds.

3. He calls the Kidron "Valley of Jehoshaphat" meaning "vale of God's judgement"

David is decisive at the Kidron: he knows he must provide leadership to his people, and leads them across the river to safety from the approaches of his son Absalom, who was masterminding a conspiracy to finish him off:

> The whole country wept aloud as all the people passed by; the king crossed the Wadi Kidron, and all the people moved on toward the wilderness ... David went up the ascent of the Mount of Olives, weeping as he went, with his head covered and walking barefoot; and all the people who were with him covered their heads and went up, weeping as they went ... The king and all the people who were with him arrived weary at the Jordan; and there he refreshed himself. (2 Sam 15:23, 30; 16:14)

David is faced with the ubiquitous choice: fight or flight? He decides to take a path avoiding conflict and confrontation, opting for the opportunity to create a space in which to take stock.

Hezekiah (reigned 715 to 686 BC) cleansed the Temple of Ahaz's pollutions. King Hezekiah called for the sanctification of the ministers of the Lord, the purification of unclean things, an invitation to all Israel and Judah to celebrate Passover in Jerusalem, and liturgical reforms. During his reforms (700 BC), as part of the ritual cleansing of the Temple, the priests removed the unclean items from the inner part of the Temple to the courts, and the Levites carried the unclean items to Wadi Kidron:

> The priests went into the inner part of the house of the Lord to cleanse it, and they brought out all the unclean things that they found in the temple of the Lord into the court of the house of the Lord; and the Levites took them and carried them out to the Wadi Kidron. (2 Chron 29:16)

Josiah the young righteous king (640–609 BC) and great grandson of Hezekiah purges the Temple of its clutter of the idols that had been placed in God's shrine by his grandfather Manasseh:

> The king commanded the high priest Hilkiah, the priests of the second order, and the guardians of the threshold, to bring out of the temple of the Lord all the vessels made for Baal, for Asherah, and for all the host of heaven; he burned them outside Jerusalem in the fields of the Kidron, and carried their ashes to Bethel ... The altars on the roof of the upper chamber of Ahaz, which the kings of Judah had made, and the altars that Manasseh had made in the two courts of the house of the Lord, he pulled down from there

and broke in pieces, and threw the rubble into the Wadi Kidron. (2 Kgs 23:4,12)

Jeremiah the prophet (655–586 BC) looks forward to the time when this valley will be renewed:

> The whole valley of the dead bodies and the ashes, and all the fields as far as the Wadi Kidron, to the corner of the Horse Gate toward the east, shall be sacred to the Lord. It shall never again be uprooted or overthrown. (Jer 31:40)

Jesus himself regularly crossed the Kidron on his way up the hillside of the Mount of Olives to stay with Mary, Martha and Lazarus at Bethany. But on the eve of his passion this becomes the locus of perhaps the greatest—and most agonized—decision-making in history . . .

JESUS AT THE BROOK KIDRON

> After Jesus had spoken these words, he went out with his disciples across the Kidron valley to a place where there was a garden, which he and his disciples entered. Now Judas, who betrayed him, also knew the place, because Jesus often met there with his disciples. (John 18:1,2)

How Jesus loved the Garden of Gethsemane on the lower slopes of the Mount of Olives—its name means "oil press"—cool shady areas and ancient olive trees giving shelter from rain and sun. We know from the Gospels (Luke 22:39) that Jesus often went to this grove, to teach, and just to spend time with his disciples. But on the night we call Maundy Thursday, the garden of fellowship becomes the place of struggle . . . a spiritual battleground. This garden is wet, not only with the night dew, but with the tears of Christ. "He offered up prayers and supplications with loud cries and silent tears" (Heb 5:7). Lane tells us: 'The reference to "cries and tears" describes prayer in a setting of crisis.'[4] Christ, a second Adam, finds himself in a garden on the eve of his passion, where he begins to un-do the mistakes of the first.

Crossing the Kidron Valley to Gethsemane after the Last Supper, Jesus enters the darkness, and "he began to be greatly distressed and troubled" (Mark 14:33). The hour of his passion is dawning. Luke tells us that "In his anguish he prayed more earnestly, and his sweat became like great drops

---

4. Lane, *Hebrews*, 81.

of blood falling down on the ground" (Luke 22:44). The Greek word translated "anguish" (NRSV) or "agony" (RSV) is *agonia* and this is the only time it is used in the New Testament. It denotes a struggle for victory, a contest, a battle with physical, mental and spiritual dimensions. Gethsemane becomes a battlefield where demons and angels are locked in combat (Luke 22:43,44). Christ's prayer in Gethsemane, in which he truly wrestles with God, and in which chalice and sword represent different and conflicting paths to take (Luke 22:42,50), invites *us* to be prepared to struggle in prayer: to struggle with decision-making, to grapple with difficult issues, to fight with temptation. But it also invites us to move from struggle to surrender, as we cry out with Christ "Not thy will, but yours be done!"

Gethsemane reminds us of the place of spiritual combat in prayer. The prayer of Gethsemane invites us to be real in prayer—with no pretending, no false pleasantries, bringing to God our painful questions, our unresolved perplexities. Sometimes in prayer we need to face our "shadow side," the darker side of our personality—our prayer will resemble Gethsemane as a place of spiritual combat and wrestling, where struggle gives way to utter surrender to the Father of love. The psalms remind us that there is a valid place in prayer for grappling with unresolved issues and doubts.[5] They also affirm to us that there is a way through them: new faith and trust can come to the surface and new creative perspectives can emerge in the prayer of struggle.

Mark uses here three powerful verbs which take us into the heart of Christ's experience. *Ekthambeisthai* means he became utterly dismayed, tormented. It can also have the sense of being astonished, astounded. *Adeemonein* conveys the sense that he was seized by horror, gripped by a very intense anguish. *Perilupos* means he is grieved, exceedingly sorrowful, heartbroken, overcome with sadness. The heavy darkness presses Jesus into the dust of the ground. What is going on here, on the banks of the Kidron? And how does it resonate with our prayer?

Jesus is standing in solidarity with all those who face their darkest hour. In this most human of scenes, Jesus is identifying with all those who through time will be crushed by their destiny and find themselves prostrate on the ground. But one fact is significant above all else. He brings his questions, doubts and fears to one he calls *Abba*. He exposes his heart's anxieties to *Abba*. In the darkness of the garden, he enters into an intimacy with the

---

5. See Pss 10, 74, 79, 106 (community laments) and Pss 13, 42, 73 (individual struggles).

Father, and, as a result of this, Gethsemane becomes a threshold, a place of crossing.

Reaching the Greatest Decision of All Time

There seems to be a triple movement involved.

First, there is a passage from attachment to bereavement. A sense of loss—a rupturing of relationships—devastates Jesus. He had delighted in the intimate company of his disciples throughout his journeys, and now, he senses, this is coming to an end. Now there is a loosening of the bonds of friendship, in one sense, a necessary detachment, for Jesus has to separate himself from even his closest disciples, and after the Easter mystery things will never be the same again. Jesus is alone. He experiences the dark depression of mourning: it is his grief work. This is what Foster calls "the prayer of relinquishment."[6] Letting go—resonating with the ancient experience of exodus and exile—is fundamental to Christian prayer. It lies at the heart of the matter. For ourselves, we need to let go of illusions, false concepts of God and self, attachments which have become less than health-giving. We need to enter the prayer of relinquishment in many different ways.

Secondly, Jesus transits from terror to trust, from agitation to composure. He comes close, humanly speaking, to falling to pieces, but moves to a fresh perspective and a renewed sense of his destiny. This enables him to face the onslaughts and attacks of the trials that night with an astonishing dignity and calm that he sustains throughout the long hours of his passion.

Thirdly, Jesus makes a passage from resistance to surrender. Looking his impending death in the face, symbolized in taking a draught from the bitter cup, Jesus prays: "Abba, Father, for you all things are possible; remove this cup from me." For a moment, he is filled with a very human sense of dread in the face of suffering. But he is able to go on "yet, not what I want, but what you want" (Mark 14:36). Slowly yet deliberately and decisively, there is an abandonment to God, a yielding, a submission, a giving in, a movement from hesitant holding back to courageous self-emptying. This is, in fact, a process of reaching the greatest decision in history. Jesus decides to embrace the Cross.

Maybe, with the murmuring sound of the Kidron Brook within earshot, Jesus saw in the stream an image of the pouring out of his life. Did he see mirrored in its waters, illuminated by the paschal full moon, his

---

6. Foster, *Prayer*, 48.

very vocation and destiny? The stream begins beside the city and flows out into the desert, bringing renewal wherever it flows. John will go on to write of the crucifixion: "one of the soldiers thrust a lance into his side, and immediately a flow of blood and water came forth" (19:34, NCB); "blood and water poured out" (GNT). John recognized this as a significant detail, writing: "This report is from an eyewitness giving an accurate account. He speaks the truth so that you also may believe" (19:35, NLT). The Kidron itself, flowing out into the wilderness, becomes a symbol of the passion.

Certainly, Jesus emerges from Gethsemane a changed man. He is able to face the coming trails and humiliation with astonishing dignity and composure. In John's Gospel, he even seems to takes charge of the situation. He has made his momentous decision: indeed a life-changing decision in the widest possible sense.

> Judas brought a detachment of soldiers together with police from the chief priests and the Pharisees, and they came there with lanterns and torches and weapons. Then Jesus, knowing all that was to happen to him, came forward and asked them, "For whom are you looking?" They answered, "Jesus of Nazareth." Jesus replied, "I am he." (John 18:3–6)

Jesus crosses the Kidron twice on the eve of passion: first as a free man going to Gethsemane and secondly as a prisoner led to Caiaphas' prison. But he is no victim of circumstance. He is a man of decision:

> I lay down my life in order to take it up again. No one takes it from me, but I lay it down of my own accord. I have power to lay it down, and I have power to take it up again. I have received this command from my Father. (John 10:17,18)

Indecision of Peter

This contrasts markedly with the behavior of Peter. He allows himself to be double-minded and pulled in two directions at once. He vacillates between wanting somehow to be close to Jesus but keeping a safe distance for his own self-preservation.

- With the noisy flow of the brook Kidron in his ears, he wants to stay awake but falls asleep: "Simon, are you asleep? Could you not watch one hour?" (Mark 14:37)

- He leaps to Jesus' defense when the armed guard arrives in the garden of Gethsemane, cutting off the ear of the high priest's servant with a sword (John 18:10) but then he hangs back.
- He wants to support Jesus but keeps a distance, warming himself by a fire while Jesus shivers in the cold courtyard.
- He denies Jesus three times saying "I do not know this man of whom you speak" (Mark 14).
- Jesus looks across the courtyard at Peter while he lurks in the shadows. He breaks down and weeps (Mark 14:72).

VOICES FROM THE RIVERBANK

St Saba: A Decision for Others in the Kidron

The Greek Orthodox monastic village of Mar Saba, dating from the fifth century and one of the oldest continually occupied monasteries in the world, and one of the most influential, has grown barnacle-like on the cliffs above the Kidron valley. It all began because of the big-hearted decisiveness of its founder St Saba (439–532). He had come to Palestine from Cappadocia seeking a life of solitary prayer. After training in the spiritual life under Euthymius the Great he spent a time with Theoctistus in the Judean desert, until he was directed by angels to the Kidron valley. Cyril of Scythopolis tells us:

> While he was praying to God through the night, there appeared to him an angelic form in dazzling apparel who showed him a gorge descending from Siloam to the south and said "If you really want to colonize this desert, stay here and ascend the east side of that gorge, where you see facing you an intact cave. Make it your home, and he who 'gives their food to the animals and to the young ravens that invoke him' will himself take care of you." So ran the vision; he, on coming to himself and observing the gorge to the south that had been indicated, descended the hill full of joy and by God's guidance found the cave just as he had been told in the vision. When he had ascended, he made it his home, at the beginning of the fortieth year of his life.[7]

---

7. Cyril, *Lives*, 106.

He continued this way of life until he was prompted to make a big decision, and indeed, turn his life around for the sake of others. He came to realize in 483 that God was calling him to sacrifice his life of solitude so he could become available to many other God-seekers:

> In this [Kidron] gorge he spent five years alone by himself in solitude, conversing with God and purifying the eye of his thought as "with unveiled face to behold as in a mirror the glory of the Lord" since the evil spirits had already been conquered by his ceaseless prayers and nearness to God. In consequence, he was now, in the forty-fifth year of his life, entrusted by God with the charge of souls; he was persuaded by the word of God not to devote time pointlessly to enemies who had been defeated but to transfer his spiritual energies from a warlike disposition to husbanding those who had grown rank with evil thoughts, for the benefit of the many, in accordance with the words of the prophet, "Beat your swords into ploughshares and your spears into pruning hooks."
> So he began to receive all those who came to him. Many of the scattered anchorites and "grazers" came to join him . . . Each of these as they came to him he provided with a suitable spot consisting of a small cell and cave. By divine grace his community grew to seventy persons, all inspired by God, all bearers of Christ; if one were to call them a choir of angels or a band of athletes or a city of the pious or a new choir of seventy apostles, one would not err in appropriateness. And he was their superior, guide, and shepherd.[8]

It was as if the Kidron, for him, changed from being a battlefield, marked by demonic conflict, into a training ground. Saba transferred his spiritual energies from struggling with demons into something that would come to influence the whole eastern Church. He moved from his cave on the eastern side of the gorge to a site opposite, where grew up an entire monastic village, safeguarded from attack by massive walls built in the sixth century in Justinian's time: today it resembles a fortress of faith in the desert. There, Saba composed the first monastic rule of church services, the so-called *Jerusalem Typikon*, for the guidance of all the Byzantine monasteries: it became the worldwide model of monastic life and liturgical order in the Byzantine rite. His Great Lavra long continued to be the most influential monastery

---

8. Cyril, *Lives*, 108.

in those parts, and produced several distinguished monks, among them St John of Damascus.[9]

The impact of the life of Saba and his exceptional system of monastic life has endured from the fifth century to the present. As the monks today at Mar Saba testify:

> The historical path of St Saba's Lavra is the fruit of the Saint's godly virtue and proof of his glory and his boldness before God . . . we recognize the impact of the monastic life of the Lavra as it became a model which played a decisive role in the formation of the monastic life and ecclesiastical order throughout the whole Church.[10]

MAKING DECISIONS

We have seen how the Kidron truly became a Valley of Decision, as exemplified by Jesus himself, St Saba and characters from the Old Testament. This river challenges us to be decisive and to leave procrastination or dithering behind.

Of course it is Ignatius of Loyola (1491–1556) who gives us clear guidelines on how we might go about making a decision that may reshape our entire vocation, or the course of our life.

He offers us two approaches,[11] beginning with six practical discernment techniques:

1. Identify and clarify the decision to be made, holding before you the very purpose of your existence: "the praise of our Lord God and my soul's salvation."

2. Be prepared to go either way: "like a pair of scales perfectly poised, inclined neither this way nor that."

3. Commit yourself to increasing the greater glory of God, asking "that of his good pleasure our Lord God may influence my will and show me what action of mine in this matter will be more to his honor and renown."

---

9. See Chitty, *Desert a City*; Binns, *Ascetics and Ambassadors*; Hirschfield, *Judean Desert Monasteries* and Patrich, *Sabas*.
10. Zisis, *Holy Lavra of Sabbas*, 45.
11. Corbishley, *Spiritual Exercises*, 178–187.

4. Carefully evaluate the pros and cons of each option—that is the "advantages and benefits" and the "dangers and disadvantages" both of the alternatives of staying unchanged or going for a change.
5. "See in what direction reason points," setting aside "natural inclinations."
6. Surrender your conclusions to God: "offering this decision to be ratified by His Divine Majesty's acceptance of it, supposing that His service and praise are thereby promoted."

There is a second complementary approach:

1. Check your motives: let the love of God be the highest priority in all things: "the love that is the motive inspiring this decision must be that higher love, deriving from the love of God."
2. Ask yourself: how would I advise a person I had never met about this?
3. Ask yourself: how would I view this decision if I looked back on it from my deathbed?
4. What would I say to God about this on Judgement Day when he makes his decision about me?

Ignatius' golden rule is this:

> "in everything we do, the one thing we aim at, the one purpose we have in mind is the greater praise and glory of our Lord God."

As we reflect on the message of the Kidron, we have encountered indecision, procrastination and big-hearted commitments. This river, flowing out from the city into the desert, summons us to be courageous and trusting in all our decision-making. We might make our own Ignatius' risky, radical *Suscipe* prayer :

> *Take, O Lord, and receive my entire liberty,*
> *my memory, my understanding and my whole will.*
> *All that I am and all that I possess You have given me.*
> *I surrender it all to You*
> *All is Yours: dispose of it wholly according to Your will.*
> *Give me only Your love and Your grace;*
> *with these I will be rich enough:*
> *I will need nothing else,*
> *desire nothing more.*

QUESTIONS FOR REFLECTION

1. What strikes you most about the challenge and invitation of the Kidron?
2. With what character do you identify most closely? Why?
3. What decisions have you made that were life-changing? How did you go about making them?
4. What kind of decisions are facing you in your life right now?
5. How do you plan to approach them?

PART TWO
Springs of Hope

Old Well at Beersheva, 1900–1920

6

ABRAHAM'S WELL, BEERSHEVA

Achieving Unexpected Reconciliation

"We have found water!"
"The water is ours." (Gen 26)

ANCIENT VOICES RICOCHET ACROSS the centuries from the environs of Abraham's Well and speak powerfully into one of the most acute issues of our own day: the struggle for water and for its control in the Holy Land and indeed across many parts of the world. As we travel south to Beersheva, located on the northern fringes of the Negev desert, we encounter a very ancient well, perhaps originating 2000 BC, that has become a poignant symbol for contemporary times. It turns out to be not only representative of humanity's thirst, physical and spiritual, but also suggestive of how we might creatively handle conflict over water supplies today.

Today the pilgrim can visit the archaeological park that reveals exciting excavations carried out at Tel Be'er Sheva from 1969 to 1976 by Tel Aviv University. The excavation uncovered an incredibly well-constructed and planned Iron Age city. The earliest strata uncovered at Tel Be'er Sheva date from the Iron Age (c. 1200–1000 BC) and as part of the city's fortifications, a large and complex water system was built into the hillside to provide water in times of siege. It is possible to walk through this system which has a 56-foot deep shaft and a large reservoir capable of holding 185,000 gallons of water. But the focus of our attention is a mysterious, more ancient well at the city gates. This may derive from the times of earliest human settlement on this fringe of the desert, the era of Abraham and Isaac.[1]

From the top of the tell one has astonishing views of the Negev desert to the south. The mound of the tell overlooks the confluence of the Hebron and Beersheva streams which drain extensive areas to the south of Mount Hebron and the northern Negev. The well that was dug on the mound through to the groundwater goes down to a depth of some 70 meters, more than twice the height of the mound itself. In his visit in 1838 Edward Robinson writes:

> The well is circular, and stoned up with solid masonry. The water is pure and sweet, and in great abundance; the finest, indeed, we had found since leaving Sinai . . . Here then is the place where the patriarchs Abraham, Isaac, and Jacob often dwelt! Here Abraham dug perhaps this very well; and journeyed from hence with Isaac to Mount Moriah, to offer him up there in sacrifice.[2]

Explorer Claude Reignier Conder adds ". . . the principal well, twelve feet three inches in diameter, is lined with rings of masonry to a depth of twenty-eight feet. The sides of the well are furrowed by the ropes of centuries of the water-drawers . . ."[3]

CONTEMPORARY REALITIES

The Desperate Clamor for Water

Jeremiah's ancient words seem so contemporary:

> Judah mourns and her gates languish;
> They lie in gloom on the ground,
> and the cry of Jerusalem goes up.
> Her nobles send their servants for water;
> they come to the cisterns;
> they find no water,
> they return with their vessels empty.
> they are ashamed and dismayed and cover their heads,
> because the ground is cracked.
> Because there has been no rain on the land

---

1. Murphy-O'Connor, *Holy Land*, 188.
2. Robinson, *Biblical Researches in Palestine*.
3. Conder, *Tent Work in Palestine*.

the farmers are dismayed;
they cover their heads (Jer 14:2–4).

The struggle for water is ancient in this land.
The story of Hagar, Abraham's concubine who gave birth to Ismael, regarded as the father of the Arab people, poignantly expresses the thirst in her story in Genesis 21 that prefaces the account of Abraham's Well:

> Abraham rose early in the morning, and took bread and a skin of water, and gave it to Hagar, putting it on her shoulder, along with the child, and sent her away. And she departed, and wandered about in the wilderness of Beersheva.
>
> When the water in the skin was gone, she cast the child under one of the bushes. Then she went and sat down opposite him a good way off, about the distance of a bowshot; for she said, "Do not let me look on the death of the child." And as she sat opposite him, she lifted up her voice and wept.
>
> And God heard the voice of the boy; and the angel of God called to Hagar from heaven, and said to her, "What troubles you, Hagar? Do not be afraid; for God has heard the voice of the boy where he is. Come, lift up the boy and hold him fast with your hand, for I will make a great nation of him." Then God opened her eyes, and she saw a well of water. She went, and filled the skin with water, and gave the boy a drink.
>
> God was with the boy, and he grew up; he lived in the wilderness, and became an expert with the bow. He lived in the wilderness of Paran; and his mother got a wife for him from the land of Egypt. (Gen 21:14–21)

This story is especially resonant because it points us to the present-day conflict between Jew and Arab, Israeli and Palestinian, both children of Abraham. We cannot proceed without reminding ourselves of the terrible disparities over water today.

Struggle for Water Today in the Holy Land

The situation is particularly stark on the occupied West Bank, both in its northern section and southern as it stretches down towards Beersheva. In 1967 most ancestral wells in the West Bank were forcibly sealed, so now Palestinians have to buy water at high cost and not use the water beneath their feet from the mountain aquifer, which lies deep in the Palestinian West Bank territory. The newly-built Separation Barrier cuts deep into the

West Bank area at Ariel in order for the Israelis to wrestle control of it from the Palestinians. Of the water from this aquifer, the Israelis use 83 per cent and the Palestinians 17 per cent. The Israelis use four times the amount per capita than the Palestinians are permitted.[4] In the summer months, when reserves are low, the Israeli water company Mekorot closes valves supplying Palestinian villages on the West Bank to safeguard supplies for the settlers. The Jewish settlers fill their swimming pools, wash their cars and water their lawns, while just a couple of miles away supplies might be cut off to Palestinian villages for essential use in cooking, sanitation and survival.

Not only have many historic West Bank Palestinian farmers' wells (in Ottoman, British and Jordanian law regarded as a private resource owned by villages) been blocked or sealed by the Israeli military, Palestinians are forbidden to drill new wells without military authorization, almost impossible to obtain. Historic wells furnishing Palestinian villages have often been expropriated for the exclusive use of Jewish settlements: near Jerusalem, the major well serving al-Eizariya (Lazaria/ Bethany) was taken over by the settlement on occupied land of Ma'ale Adumin, which has swollen to a population of 40 thousand. Amnesty International reports: "Some 180 Palestinian communities in rural areas in the occupied West Bank have no access to running water, according to the United Nations Office for the Coordination of Humanitarian Affairs (OCHA). Even in towns and villages connected to the water network, the taps often run dry . . . The World Health Organization's (WHO) recommended daily minimum per person is 100 liters: in many herding communities in the West Bank, the water consumption for thousands of Palestinians is as low as 20 liters per person a day, according to OCHA. By contrast, an average Israeli consumes approximately 300 liters of water a day."[5]

The struggle for water is a daily reality in the occupied territories. Nabi Salih is a small Palestinian village in the central West Bank, located 20 kilometers northwest of Ramallah. Near the village there is a natural spring named Ein al-Qaws, "the Bow Spring," bubbling up from a low, stone cliff and owned by an individual of the village, Bashir Tamimi. In 2009 settlers from the nearby illegal Israeli settlement of Halamish took control over the spring and its surroundings and prevented Palestinian access to their land. The settlers renamed the spring Meier's Spring, after one of the settlement's

---

4. Three million Palestinians use 250 million cubic meters a year, while six million Israelis use 2000 million cubic meters, according to palestinemonitor.org

5. Amnesty, "Occupation of Water."

founders, and created a concrete pool and a recreation area. When the owner and Palestinian residents came to tend their fields nearby, they were beaten and threatened by the armed settlers. Subsequently, people of Nabi Salih began regular Friday protests for the spring, and against the Israeli occupation in general: they are frequently wounded by the army's rubber-coated metal bullets and tear gas. Ben Ehrenreich's *The Way to the Spring: Life and Death in Palestine* chronicles the daily humiliations and acts of resistance to the theft of the spring. There are other examples.[6]

It is with these contexts in mind that we turn to the biblical accounts of Abraham's Well.

BIBLICAL CONFLICTS OVER WATER AT BEERSHEVA

Abraham and Abimelech

> At that time Abimelech, with Phicol the commander of his army, said to Abraham, "God is with you in all that you do; now therefore swear to me here by God that you will not deal falsely with me or with my offspring or with my posterity, but as I have dealt loyally with you, you will deal with me and with the land where you have resided as an alien." And Abraham said, "I swear it."
>
> When Abraham complained to Abimelech about a well of water that Abimelech's servants had seized, Abimelech said, "I do not know who has done this; you did not tell me, and I have not heard of it until today." So Abraham took sheep and oxen and gave them to Abimelech, and the two men made a covenant. Abraham set apart seven ewe lambs of the flock. And Abimelech said to Abraham, "What is the meaning of these seven ewe lambs that you have set apart?" He said, "These seven ewe lambs you shall accept from my hand, in order that you may be a witness for me that I dug this well." Therefore that place was called Beersheva; because there both of them swore an oath. When they had made a covenant at Beersheva, Abimelech, with Phicol the commander of his army, left and returned to the land of the Philistines. Abraham planted a tamarisk tree in Beersheva, and called there on the name of the Lord, the Everlasting God. And Abraham resided as an alien for many days in the land of the Philistines. (Gen 21:21–34)

---

6. Ehrenreich, *Way to the Spring*. See also Starr, *Middle Eastern Waters*; Selby, *The Other Israel-Palestine Conflict*.

In Genesis 21:25–34 we read of Abraham's argument with the Canaanite warlord Abimelech, whose servants seized control of a well of water Abraham was using. Abraham resolves the dispute and avoids further conflict by entering into a covenant with Abimelech, sealing the agreement by his gift to him of seven lambs, which gives the well the name Beersheva, meaning "the well of the oath."

Isaac and Abimelech

Some time later Abraham's son Isaac also comes face to face with Abimelech, in a passage which replays close study, Genesis 26:14–33.

> Isaac had possessions of flocks and herds, and a great household, so that the Philistines envied him. Now the Philistines had stopped up and filled with earth all the wells that his father's servants had dug in the days of his father Abraham. And Abimelech said to Isaac, "Go away from us; you have become too powerful for us."
> So Isaac departed from there and camped in the valley of Gerar and settled there. Isaac dug again the wells of water that had been dug in the days of his father Abraham; for the Philistines had stopped them up after the death of Abraham; and he gave them the names that his father had given them. But when Isaac's servants dug in the valley and found there a well of spring water, the herders of Gerar quarreled with Isaac's herders, saying, "The water is ours." So he called the well Esek [*Contention*], because they contended with him. Then they dug another well, and they quarreled over that one also; so he called it Sitnah [*Enmity*]. He moved from there and dug another well, and they did not quarrel over it; so he called it Rehoboth [*Broad places*], saying, "Now the Lord has made room for us, and we shall be fruitful in the land."
> From there he went up to Beersheva. And that very night the Lord appeared to him and said, "I am the God of your father Abraham; do not be afraid, for I am with you and will bless you and make your offspring numerous for my servant Abraham's sake." So he built an altar there, called on the name of the Lord, and pitched his tent there. And there Isaac's servants dug a well.
> Then Abimelech went to him from Gerar, with his adviser and the commander of his army. Isaac said to them, "Why have you come to me, seeing that you hate me and have sent me away from you?" They said, "We see plainly that the Lord has been with you; so we say, let there be an oath between you and us, and let us make a covenant with you so that you will do us no harm, just

> as we have not touched you and have done to you nothing but good and have sent you away in peace. You are now the blessed of the Lord." So he made them a feast, and they ate and drank. In the morning they rose early and exchanged oaths; and Isaac set them on their way, and they departed from him in peace. That same day Isaac's servants came and told him about the well that they had dug, and said to him, "We have found water!" He called it Shibah [oath], therefore the name of the city is Beersheva [*well of the oath*] to this day.

It vividly illustrates the scramble for water in this thirsty land. Isaac's servants dug a well but Abimelech's herdsmen protest in words that are heard today in this same land: "The water is *ours!*" (Gen 26:20). Isaac refuses to give into fear and intimidation and moves on, sinking another well at a distance (but no doubt using the same underground watertable). Ultimately Isaac enters into a covenant with Abimelech (Gen 26:31), a relationship based on mutual respect and mutual interest—former foes sit and eat and drink (water?) together as they seal a pact and exchange oaths. That same day Isaac's servants come to him rejoicing and say "We have found water!" As Isaac observes (Gen 26:22), there is room in the land for both groups, and there is enough water for all.

FORGING COVENANTS

The way forward from dispute and struggle is by way of covenant and mutual trust. The lessons shout to us from ancient Beersheva! In these narratives, the settlement between the warring parties is not called a treaty or a pact but is honored with the designation *berith*—a term that resonates and reverberates with the covenants or sacred agreements made between God and his people at Sinai and in other places. It accrues more meaning than a pragmatic truce. A covenant has a sacred quality and its fulfilment should be characterized by *hesed*—loyalty, deep faithfulness. William J. Everett puts it succinctly:

> The idea of covenant points the way in which new relationships, not rooted in the inevitability of repeating communally inherited habits of hatred and cycles of revenge, are forged through intentional acts of entrustment.[7]

---

7. Quoted in de Gruchy, *Reconciliation*, 185.

The covenants over the sharing of water supplies and over respecting different claims of wells give testimony that differing factions, indeed differing ethnicities, have the capacity for entering into relationships that have the potential to transform suspicion into trust. Of course a key biblical theme is reconciliation and the overcoming of estrangement—between God and humanity, and between different peoples. But another significant theme emerges here.

Taking a Leap of Faith

Abraham makes a leap of faith. He seizes the initiative, offering sheep and oxen to Abimelech. He could just have resigned himself to the status quo of ongoing tension and conflict—and unresolved thirst. But Abraham lives as a person of faith and responds to situations with bigheartedness. He stands as a paradigm for all followers of monotheistic religions, for Christians, Jews and Muslims are all children of Abraham: "those who have faith are blessed along with Abraham, the man of faith" (Gal 3:9 EHV). When faced with situations of division, Abraham teaches us, it is sometimes necessary to take the risk, face the danger of rejection, but steadfastly reach out towards the Other.

Learning to Share?

It was at Beersheva that Ben Gurion, the first president of the State of Israel, promised to turn the desert into a rose. Here, where a university now exists in his name, he recalled the hope of the prophet Isaiah: "The desert shall rejoice, and blossom as the rose." Indeed, these words have come true: it was in this region of the Negev that Israelis developed the pioneering drip system of irrigation, which has spread across the globe. But the question remains: how can we share what we have? Environmental scientist Daniel Hillel puts it:

> The hydrological imperative presents a challenge and an opportunity. Water can catalyze and lubricate the peace process, smooth the rough edges, and soften the transition to regional cooperation. The thirst for water may be more persuasive than the impulse towards conflict. For the people of the Middle East, who have lost faith in empty promises, peace will be more attractive if it offers

tangible prospects for progress and prosperity, first and foremost in the development and equitable sharing of water supplies.⁸

As we noted in chapter 4, the Israeli and Jordanian governments signed at the UN COP27 a declaration of intent on 27 November 2022 to partner in the ecological restoration and clean up of the polluted Jordan River. It is not quite a covenant, but a step along the way. More are needed.

VOICES FROM THE SPRING

RESOURCING RECONCILIATION

Covenant-making and reconciliation require deep reserves of patience, attentiveness to the Other, graciousness and generosity of spirit. How are we to locate such reserves? The image of Abraham and Isaac digging their wells is suggestive: we must ourselves dig down deep to find what is necessary for the challenge. There are two phrases in the writings of St Bernard of Clairvaux (1090–1153) that resonate strongly with this.

"We Drink From Our Own Wells"

This striking phrase echoes the proverb: "Drink water from your own cistern, And fresh water from your own well" (Prov 5:15 NASB). Bernard wrote:

> Spiritual life is like living water that springs up from the very depths of our own spiritual experience. In spiritual life everyone has to drink from his or her own well.⁹

Bernard is telling us that we must take responsibility for our own spirituality that will become the wellspring of mission, and he reminds us that we do not have to look very far, for it springs from our context and setting. Indeed, if it is divorced from contemporary concerns about our environment, for example, it will prove fruitless. This phrase is picked by the great liberation theologian Gustavo Gutierrez in his pioneering book on the spirituality evolving from struggles in Latin America, *We Drink from Our Own Wells: The Spiritual Journey of a People*.¹⁰ Henri Nouwen explains: "To

---

8. Hillel, *Rivers of Eden*, 283.
9. Bernard of Clairvaux, "De Consideration", II, 1, 2.
10. Gutierrez, *We Drink from Our Own Wells*.

drink from your own well is to live your own life in the Spirit of Jesus as you have encountered him in your concrete historical reality."[11]

Before we can drink, we need to dig our wells. We need to locate the hidden sources of the Spirit that lie, as it were, beneath our very feet. Meister Eckhart affirms: "God is a great underground river that no one can dam up and no one can stop."[12] The Divine is not far away.

The concept of depth is becoming more frequent in contemporary spirituality.[13] Paul Tillich in his ground-breaking study *The Shaking of the Foundations* invites us to rediscover the metaphor of the depths of God:

> Most of our life continues on the surface. We are enslaved by the routine of our daily lives . . . We are in constant motion and never stop to plunge into the depth. We talk and talk and never listen to the voices speaking to our depth and from our depth . . . It is comfortable to live on the surface . . . It is painful to break away from it and to descend into an unknown ground.[14]

We are summoned to quit superficial living and risk a descent into the depths, where we may find God and in the process, rediscover ourselves. Richard Foster puts it: "Superficiality is the curse of our age . . . The desperate need today is not for a greater number of intelligent people, or gifted people, but for deep people."[15] In his book *Contemplative Prayer*, Merton writes "Prayer begins with a return to the heart, finding one's deepest center, awakening the profound depths of our being." In another place he affirms: "The things on the surface are nothing, what is deep is the Real."[16] David Anderson writes:

> I love that image of God because it completely flips the dominant image of God "up there." When we first imagine a deity, God is always "up," always distant, the Sky God of nearly every ancient religion. Until gradually it dawns upon us that the God whom the cosmos cannot contain is actually deep within. The ground of our being. And that underground river runs right through you. Sink a well within yourself and in the hidden darkness of your soul

---

11. Nouwen, "Foreword" in Gutierrez, *We Drink*, xiv.

12. Fox, *Meditations with Meister Eckhart*, 16.

13. See, for example, Mayes, *Centre of the Soul*; Raguin, *Depth of God*; Mary Clare, *Encountering the Depths*; Ramon, *Deeper into God*.

14. Tillich, *Shaking*, ch. 7.

15. Foster, *Celebration of Discipline*, 1.

16. Cunningham, *Thomas Merton*, 237.

> the river erupts. Water! Through the prophet God promises even "streams in the desert." God is the subterranean gusher and prayer is the well. Draw deeply—and often.[17]

The image of Abraham and Isaac digging their wells in the harsh desert soils and rocks of the Negev at Beersheva gives us a powerful encouragement to take up, as it were, a spade into our own hands . . . We need to look beyond the rubble and the dirt that clutters the surface. We won't focus on the dirt to be removed, but on the water to be received. We need to pray for the grace to be resolute and determined. We need to break ground—to begin somewhere, no matter how small our efforts may seem at first. We must dig deep to locate water. The ground may be hard, others may give up, but we must stay and persevere. This choice will confront us again and again.

We must remain constant in expectant prayer, ever on the lookout for hidden signs of the Divine revealing themselves, clues to God's presence in our very midst. A new attentiveness is required of us: a sharpness and alertness of spirit that notices where God is, and does not miss God.

"Love like a River Overflows and Floods the Lands"

In his great work *On The Love of God*, Bernard of Clairvaux has much to say about love and attentiveness to the needs of our neighbors.

> Let a man think of himself as much as ever he will, if only he take care to think equally of his neighbor.
> If you heed the counsel of the wise, you will turn away from your own appetites and discipline yourself (Prov 13:18). Then you will follow the teaching of the apostle: "But if we have food and clothing, we will be content with that" (1 Tim 6:8). Then you will not find it a burden to share with your neighbor what you have held back from the enemy of your soul [selfish passions] . . . So what could readily be a selfish love can become truly social when it can extend to include others.[18]

Bernard asks: but what if, in sharing with others, your own reserves become depleted?

> But if you find that your benevolence to your neighbor reduces your own support which you personally need, what can you do

---

17. Anderson, "God is an underground river."
18. Bernard of Clairvaux, *On the Love of God*.

then? . . . "Ask God who gives generously to all without finding fault, and it will be given to you" (James 1:5). Again, as the psalmist says, "You open your hand and satisfy the desires of every living thing" (Ps 145:16). There is no doubt that God will provide for our needs; indeed, He gives most people more than they need. So His promise is true: "Seek first the Kingdom of God and His righteousness, and all these things will be given to you as well" (Matt 6:33). God freely promises to give all things necessary to those who do not withhold themselves from the needs of others and who thus love their neighbors. To seek first the Kingdom of God means to prefer the yoke of modesty and sobriety with God's help . . .

Bernard has practical advice for dealing with neighbors:

> Do not judge rashly. If you hear evil of any one, do not hasten to judge your neighbor, but excuse him if you can. Excuse the intention if you cannot the action. Think that he did it in ignorance, or by misfortune, or was surprised into doing it, or, at most, that perhaps the temptation was exceedingly strong; and say to yourself, What should I have done under like pressure?

The question remains: what spiritual reserves are we finding in the well of our prayer and spirituality? Bernard is clear:

> If we are to love our neighbor with absolute righteousness, we need to acknowledge God as our motive and cause. For how can we love with pure motives if we do not love God first of all? Only then can we love our neighbor. It is impossible to love in God without first loving God (1 Thess 2:1–11). So it is essential we love God first in order to love others also. God, as the source of all goodness, is the source of our ability and disposition to love others . . . In order that love for our neighbor be entirely right, God must have His part in it; it is not possible to love our neighbor as we ought to do, except in God. Those that love not God can love nothing in Him. We must therefore begin by loving God, and so love our neighbor in Him.

In Bernard's teaching, respect for the needs of neighbors, and self-respect represent the most basic of his four degrees of love. The highest form of love—that which makes reconciliation possible and energizes it—is love of God for his sake. He expresses this in his hymns:

> Jesus, thou joy of loving hearts!
> Thou fount of life! Thou Light of all!
> From the best bliss that earth imparts,

> We turn unfill'd to Thee again.
>
> We taste thee, O thou living Bread,
> And long to feast upon thee still!
> We drink of Thee the Fountain-head,
> And thirst our souls from thee to fill!

His beautiful hymn, "Jesus the Very Thought of Thee," reverberates with the language of divine love.

> O hope of every contrite heart,
> O joy of all the meek,
> to those who ask how kind thou art,
> how good to those who seek!
>
> But what to those who find? Ah, this
> nor tongue nor pen can show;
> the love of Jesus, what it is
> none but his loved ones know. [19]

And with those words, I will, as advised, lay down my pen!

QUESTIONS FOR REFLECTION

1. Jesus says "Whoever gives even a cup of cold water to one of these little ones in the name of a disciple—truly I tell you, none of these will lose their reward" (Matt 10:42). How far are you prepared to share your own resources—with family, friends, neighbors, strangers? What holds you back?

2. Can you think of a situation of conflict where a "leap of faith" might bridge the divide? Learning from the story of Abraham's Well, how might that happen?

3. What spiritual resources do you have to share with those who are spiritually thirsty in your midst?

4. How aware are you of the physical thirst in the peoples of the Holy Land?

5. How aware are you of your own spiritual thirst?

---

19. Both hymns from *Hymns Ancient and Modern*.

Mary's Well 1910

7

MARY'S WELL, NAZARETH

Encountering the Divine in the Everyday

In the sixth month the angel Gabriel was sent by God
to a town in Galilee called Nazareth (Luke 1:26)

AT THE TIME OF Jesus Nazareth was a hamlet of 200 souls nestling in the hills, with the well at the very center of the community, indeed its beating heart. The village sat above a broad valley which drops steeply away southwards (the Mount of Precipice). The tiny, off-the-beaten-path hamlet was framed by hills above it, and the spring gushed from the base of the hills. It grew as it became a pilgrimage site, and in the 19th century Europeans built many convents and orphanages. Gradually the village turned into the sprawling modern Arab Israeli city we find today, as it blossomed as a center of commerce.

Noise!

Among Nazareth's environmental problems is the issue of noise pollution. The visitor to Nazareth today is assaulted by a cacophony of sound. The roads are choked with traffic: piercing car horns in clogged, congested streets; shouting of traders; grinding of industrial machines and scream and screech of earth-movers, the hammer of building works intensifying already dense urban development. Punctuating the row are the regular call of the muezzin and the clanging of angelus bells. Different sounds clamor for attention—it is as if they are in competition with each other amidst the business and busyness of the city. Today Nazareth is a vibrant Arab town, a center of commerce and the largest Arab city in the state of Israel with a population of 80 thousand of whom 70% are Muslim and 40% Christian.

Broodingly strategically above the city from the top of the hill is the largely Jewish immigrant town of Upper Nazareth (Nazareth Illit, known as Nof HaGalil) with a population of 45 thousand. (A fifth of the residents are Arab but the municipality refuses to allow the building of any churches, mosques or Arabic-speaking schools). The function of the upper town is to block the natural development of the lower, original Arab town below and to assert Israeli supremacy over the area. Unfortunately the upper town also creates a bottleneck of horn-blaring traffic jams in driving north to Zepphoris...

Where did Mary meet the Angel?

Luke's gospel does not reveal the location of the Annunciation, but the second century *Protoevangelium of James* gives us this account:

> And Mary took the pitcher, and went out to fill it with water. And, behold, a voice saying: "Hail, you who hast received grace; the Lord is with you; blessed are you among women!" And she looked round, on the right hand and on the left, to see whence this voice came.
>
> And she went away, trembling, to her house, and put down the pitcher; and taking the purple, she sat down on her seat, and drew it out. And, behold, an angel of the Lord stood before her, saying: "Fear not, Mary; for you have found grace before the Lord of all, and you shall conceive, according to His word." And she hearing, reasoned with herself, saying: "Shall I conceive by the Lord, the living God? And shall I bring forth as every woman brings forth?" And the angel of the Lord said: "Not so, Mary; for the power of the Lord shall overshadow you: wherefore also the holy One which shall be born of you shall be called the Son of the Most High. And you shall call His name Jesus, for He shall save His people from their sins."
>
> And Mary said: "Behold, the servant of the Lord before His face: let it be unto me according to your word."

Thus two traditions about the physical location of the Annunciation compete for pilgrims' attention in Nazareth today. Western Christians follow the Latin, Franciscan tradition and recall the awesome visitation of the angel in the home of Mary. The cave of Mary's home is preserved under the copula of the Basilica built in 1966—paradoxically the largest church in the Middle East sits above the tiny humble cave. The message of this church is that Mary received the angel while alone at home, at work, according to the symbolism of the *Protoevangelium*, weaving a curtain for the Jerusalem Temple's Holy of Holies.

But Eastern Christians make their way to Mary's Well. At the center of the traditional town a spring bubbles up beneath an oft-restored stone arch. Mary's Well has been the main water source for the town since Roman times, and a buzzling focal point of social life. In the Bible, of course, the local well is the place of meeting and encounter: patriarchs meet their future wives at wells: Isaac's agent meets Rebekah (Gen 24:11–21), Jacob encounters Rachel (Gen 29:1–13), and Moses meets Zipporah (Exod 2:15–22).

But a few yards behind it, across the square, an evocative spring gurgles in an ancient crypt. Within the Greek Orthodox Church of St Gabriel, pilgrims descend several steps, past glistening walls decorated by Armenian tiles, to where the original well of Nazareth was located. In fact the water originates from a spring just behind the church which archaeologists uncovered in 1979. The water is sweet and refreshing on a hot day, and visitors may take a sample as both an act of devotion and as a needful taste of refreshment.

Two Traditions—One Message

Notice the contrast in the two traditions. One places Mary firstly at the noisy well, where, amidst the chattering of local women drawing water and sharing news, Mary somehow catches the whisper of the Angel. Here Mary finds herself in a public space. But the second tradition places Mary in a place of privacy and seclusion—her own home, as she weaves cloth.

Either way, Mary finds the Divine in the midst of activity, at the center of her daily tasks, at the core of her work. Either way Mary is working when she encounters the Angel, not resting. Mary will, indeed, prove herself to be a natural contemplative, ready to encounter God in the midst of the daily round. She is not alternating stillness and movement so much as learning the challenge to be a contemplative in action: to bring a contemplative listening discerning heart into the midst of situations of work, labor and social interaction.

Becoming a Contemplative in Action:

Finding God Amidst the Noise

At the Annunciation, Mary, a teenager of sixteen years according to the *Protoevangelium*, is invited to take part in God's plan for the world. She is greeted by God's messenger Gabriel with the words: "Rejoice, O full of grace, the Lord is with you." Mary is not only surprised at these words (Luke 1:29) but she is disturbed, troubled, perturbed—the Greek means "thrown into great confusion, confounded." She tries to work out what has actually been said to her. Gabriel tells her not to be afraid— so what fears are rising in her heart? What anxieties are surfacing as she senses that God is calling her to something new?

Perhaps she is overwhelmed by a sense of utter unworthiness—"Why me? What part can an uneducated young woman from an insignificant village possibly have to play in God's plans?" Coupled with this is maybe a feeling that she is not qualified or talented enough for what is to come. Such fears certainly rise in our hearts when we are faced with a new challenge. We allow ourselves to entertain a fear of failure. We ask: What if I let other people down? What if I do not measure up to their expectations? Most of all, we fear rejection. What if I make a fool of myself, and people don't appreciate me? We also face a fear of the unknown—what is God demanding of me? What risks and sacrifices lie ahead? How will it affect my family? Will I need to move house? What will I have to give up? What will I have to take on?

We can identify with Mary in her moment of hesitation and timidity as she faces up to her own fears. By her open response to God's call, revealing her anxieties to him, Mary teaches us that such fears need to be expressed in prayer. In prayer, in sharing our heart's torments and questionings with God, they can be transformed. There we will recapture the confidence of Paul: "I am sure that he who began a good work in you will bring it to completion at the day of Jesus Christ" (Phil 1:6). In prayer we gain the reassurance of Paul: "He who calls you is faithful, and he will do it" (1 Thess 5:24). But first, fears must be expressed and surrendered into God's hands, or else they will swamp us and paralyze us into inaction. Anxiety expends and burns up vital energy. It must be decisively given over to God. Slowly, gradually, fear turns to faith. This was Mary's experience.

But not before she brings her questionings before God. Luke's account shows us how she meets with God in all honesty, in her fragility and human weakness. God unfolds his hopes that she will take part in his awesome plan for the world, and invites her to become mother of the Messiah. Mary responds with an agonizing question which echoes and resounds across the centuries? "How? How can this be?" It is our question too, when we sense that God is prompting us, urging us, into some new task. How can we cope? How will we manage? How will it all work out? How will we possibly be able to meet the challenges ahead?

If Mary's question is our question, the answer given to Mary is offered to us too: "The Holy Spirit will come upon you, and the power of the Most High will overshadow you . . . For with God nothing will be impossible" (Luke 1:35,36). Mary is invited to drink deep of the living waters of the Holy Spirit. She is promised that the divine Spirit will energize, fortify and sustain her. She is reassured that seeming impossibilities will be transformed into God's opportunities. With this encouragement, all resistance and hesitation in Mary begins to melt away. She begins to relax. She has stumbled on the very heart of the Gospel, the secret of the Christian life.

The Christian faith is not supposed to be a DIY religion. We are not meant to struggle on alone, in our own efforts. We are called, rather, to surrender ourselves to God and permit him to work in our lives. The Christian vocation is a partnership with God. We are invited to be co-workers with God himself. Until we wake up to the reality of the Holy Spirit overshadowing us, we will never make sense of our vocation. Until we dare to open ourselves, with the vulnerability of Mary, to the Holy Spirit, the secret of the Christian life will pass us by. The promise made to Mary is repeated to disciples in every generation, for it is the promise of the Risen Christ to the Church: "You shall receive power when the Holy Spirit comes upon you" (Acts 1:8). Paul, too, is emphatic, crying out: "Wake up! Don't you realize?" He stirs the Corinthians with the words: "Do you not know that you are God's temple and that God's Spirit dwells in you?" (1 Cor 3:16). We need to move beyond academic assent to this proposition and actually experience it—and, like Mary, grow in our awareness and consciousness that God is not only "out there" but actually "within." We need, like Mary, to thirst for the Spirit instead of craving for success, to long for the Spirit in place of succumbing to anxiety. We need to glimpse God's own longing to give us the Spirit, and to remind ourselves of Christ's words: "If you then, who are evil, know how to give good gifts to your children, how much more will the heavenly Father give the Holy Spirit to those who ask him!" (Luke 11:13).

Through her struggle at the Annunciation, Mary gives us a vision of how things can be when we allow God to work on the raw material of human lives and when we release ourselves from the prisons and limitations of our own making. She shows us that it is possible to break free from the strait-jackets we create by entertaining fears and persisting in narrow views of what God can do. She reminds us of the supreme Christian vocation— to be a channel, a vehicle, an instrument of God's Holy Spirit in the world. The dawning realization that the Holy Spirit will overshadow her, gives Mary the courage and big-heartedness to say "Yes" to God. The promise of the Spirit moves Mary on from fear to trust, and to a point where she can surrender herself totally and without reserve to God. It is still an enormous risk, a gamble, a leap of faith. That is the character of faith: to be able to step out into the unknown and say with Mary "I am the servant of the Lord. Let it be to me according to your word" (Luke 1:38).

Pondering in the Heart

At the well—and in her home—Mary comes to realize that she is being called to become a contemplative in action, attentive to the Divine whispering in the midst of noise and activity. Luke goes on to show us how this unfolds for her.

As Jesus is born and shepherds kneel in adoration, reporting an apparition of angels in the sky overhead, Mary struggles to make sense of it all. She asks herself what is happening to her, and what it all really means. She is learning already to share her child with complete strangers. She is at once delighted and puzzled by what the shepherds have to say. Luke notes carefully: "But Mary kept all these things, pondering them in her heart" (2:19). In the very midst of the hectic and excited comings and goings at the cave of the nativity she is discovering the prayer of contemplation, in which we come before God with all our confusions and hopes and surrender ourselves totally to God. In the center of activity Mary creates a pool of stillness. It is the experience of exposing to God the hidden depths of our hearts. It is also the experience of learning to receive healing from God and invigorating love, which alone can make us whole.

Mary's Well, Nazareth

The Greek word translated "pondering" is rich in meaning. It denotes a "coming together" as in a bringing together, a uniting of different rivers. Mary is reconciling in her heart different streams of thought. She is wrestling with the paradoxes thrown up by Christ, who is at once very human and yet divine, her own child yet the redeemer of the world, born not in a palace but in the poverty of a stable. The Greek verb "pondering" can mean collecting up disparate elements, bring them into some sort of unity. It can also mean, generally, to play one's part, to contribute of one's own goods. All these meanings converge in Mary's prayer of contemplation, as she seeks to pull together conflicting forces, the desire to protect her child and the need to share him. Her hopes and her fears are beginning to meet. She is discovering the particular part God wants her to play and is coming to terms with what she must contribute. Luke conveys to us the agonizing that Mary is facing, which develops slowly into a clearer sense of purpose, a wholeness emerging out of fragmented impressions of what is happening to her. But it is not always possible to reconcile seeming contradictions. Mary is also learning to hold the paradoxes of her vocation within a creative tension.

When, forty days later, Simeon greets the Christ Child at the steps of the temple (Luke 2:25–38), she is overcome by his joy and sense of expectancy. Luke records: "And the child's mother and father were amazed at what was said about him" (2:33). He repeats the same word used to describe Mary's reaction to the shepherds (2:18)—conveying a sense of utter astonishment, even bewilderment. Mary is dumbfounded by it all. And then she hears the eerie prophecy of Simeon: "A sword will pierce your own soul too" (2:35). Mary is being prepared for indescribable suffering.

Twelve years later, Mary finds herself once again at the temple courts. After completing a family pilgrimage to Jerusalem, Mary leaves the city without her son. She presumes that Jesus will return home with the rest of the party. It is to be a rude awakening for Mary, a hard lesson to learn. She is wrong. Things are changing now. Jesus is different now; he is no longer her little boy— he has come of age. Luke reports: "When they saw him they were astonished" (2:48). Luke's Greek word conveys the sense of being absolutely astounded, even panic-struck, frightened out of one's senses. Jesus explains: "Did you not know that I must be in my Father's house?" Luke puts it bluntly: "They did not understand." (2:49).

Here Luke reveals something of the inner turmoil and confusion of Mary. She is learning that she must let go of her son. She is learning that he has a mission: to be about his divine Father's business. But she is also discovering that her own vocation must evolve. She is now longer parent to a small child; her role is changing. The nurturing and protecting is over, and her job will be different. She does not immediately understand. This is a painful time of transition for her. But the key thing is this— Luke tells us how Mary comes to understand what is happening to her: "His mother treasured all these things in her heart" (2:51). Luke's word "treasured" means "to watch closely, to keep safe." In the midst of confusion and noise she guards these events and impressions in her heart—in the deepest place of her being—the place where she can receive God's peace. In the midst of comings and goings, she again rediscovers the prayer of contemplation as a place where we come to live with the paradoxes and dilemmas of our life.

When things happen to us that are outside our control, when there is a need to let go of something or someone we are deeply attached to, we need to learn with Mary to convert anxiety into prayer. It is there that we catch a glimpse of the divine perspective and rediscover the divine empowering of the Holy Spirit. It is in prayer that we sense that God is nudging us onto the next stage of our life's vocation. Sometimes, like Mary, we will realize that our calling must undergo a metamorphosis. Our role may be changing, and relationships and expectations need adjusting. This entails inner struggle as we learn with Mary to grieve for the passing of old ways and discover the courage to embrace the new. Such transitions, such reflections, take place in the thick of it all—not necessarily in the place of retreat but in the place of engagement with changing realities. This is what it means to be a contemplative in action: discovering divine meanings and presences in the midst of the everyday. Two French spiritual writers can help us to unpack this further.

VOICES FROM THE SPRING

Jean-Pierre de Caussade

In his great classic *Self-Abandonment to Divine Providence*, de Caussade (1675–1751) encourages us to abide in a state of surrender to God.[1] De Caussade urged his readers to strive for a synergy, an active co-operation with God's will: "We know that in all things God works for good for those

---

1. He countered the Quietism heresy of fostering utter passivity before God, with complete withdrawal from the world, annihilation of human will, cessation of all human effort, to become totally available to God.

who love him, who are called according to his purpose" (Rom 8:28). De Caussade believed that God is supremely active in the world, guiding all things according to his divine plans. Our part is to be awake and responsive to God's actions, to allow him to move and direct our life in the midst of change. We are to train ourselves to recognize God's hand of providence in the "chances and changes of this mortal life."

De Caussade gave us the striking phrase "the sacrament of the present moment." He teaches us that we should not live in the past nor become anxious about the future, but rather be totally available to God this day and this very moment: "See, now is the acceptable time; see, now is the day of salvation" (2 Cor 6:2). Today, right now, God waits to meet us. De Caussade urges us to live in an attitude of continual surrender to God, yielding ourselves totally to him without qualification or preconditions, so we can become channels through which he can work: "Loving, we wish to be the instrument of his action so that his love can operate in and through us."[2] We are to live by humble trust in God, confident that he is working his purposes out. We are not to seek our own fulfilment but God's Kingdom: "Follow your path without a map, not knowing the way, and all will be revealed to you. Seek only God's kingdom and his justice through love and obedience, and all will be granted to you."[3] Abandoned into God's hands, we are to "go with the flow" as he opens and closes doors before us.

But what if suffering and upheavals come our way—can these be welcomed as God's will for us? Should we not try to fight against them? De Caussade warns that we must not set bounds or limits to God's plans. He is a "God of surprises." He works in unpredictable and unlikely ways and we should be ready for anything: "The terrifying objects put in our way are nothing. They are only summoned to embellish our lives with glorious adventures."[4] Hardships can be in God's hands pathways to growth: "With God, the more we seem to loose, the more we gain. The more he takes from us materially, the more he gives spiritually."[5] We should not resent difficult circumstances, but rather listen to what God is saying to us through them.

How then is it possible to cultivate an attitude of such openness to God? De Caussade affirms that it is achieved by living in communion with God, and allowing Jesus Christ to dwell at the very center of our being.

2. Muggeridge, *Present Moment*, 46.
3. Muggeridge, *Present Moment*, 75.
4. Muggeridge, *Present Moment*, 40.
5. Muggeridge, *Present Moment*, 54.

The Christ who longs to live within us is "noble, loving, free, serene, and fearless."⁶ De Caussade has a vision of the Christ-life growing within each person who has the courage to surrender to him. This is the secret of welcoming the fruit of "the sacrament of the present moment":

> The mysterious growth of Jesus Christ in our heart is the accomplishment of God's purpose, the fruit of his grace and divine will. This fruit forms, grows and ripens in the succession of our duties to the present which are continually being replenished by God, so that obeying them is always the best we can do. We must offer no resistance and abandon ourselves to his divine will in perfect trust.⁷

Charles de Foucauld

De Foucauld (1858–1916), canonized as a saint in 2022, lived in Nazareth (1898–1900) in his search to fathom the meaning of the Incarnation and to experience the humility and poverty of Jesus. He noted Luke's words: "Jesus *went down* with them to Nazareth" (Luke 2:51). Charles was inebriated by the image of Jesus the Worker in his so-called "hidden years." He was absorbed by the earthy idea of God in the dust and dirt of a poor town, the Divine in the everyday. He trod the narrow dirty Nazareth streets and worked hard in the gardens for the Poor Clares while assisting them as odd-job man and sacristan. Each day he spent long hours in front of the Blessed Sacrament reserved in the Franciscan chapel but as he rejoiced in the presence of Christ in this Eucharistic presence, he also learned to trace the features of Jesus in the faces of those who suffer. The sacrament of the altar pointed him to the sacrament of the poor. The two calls, contemplative and apostolic, became one, integrated, fused, as he found and honored the same Jesus in broken Bread and broken lives. He learnt the art of glimpsing Christ in the wounded and hurting: "To be able to truly see others, we must close our physical eyes and open the eyes of our souls. Let us see what they are from within, not what they appear to be. Let us look at them as God looks at them . . . See Jesus in all people."⁸

Shortly before his death he wrote to a friend:

---

6. Muggeridge, *Present Moment*, 109.
7. Muggeridge, *Present Moment*, 111.
8. Thurston, *Hidden in God*, 99.

> I think there is no saying in the Gospel that made a deeper impression on me and more transformed my life than this one: "Whatsoever you did to one of the least of these my brothers and sisters you did it to me" (Matt 25). If we remember that these are the words of Uncreated Truth and come from the same lips that said "This is my Body, This is my Blood" how compellingly are we moved to seek out Jesus and love him in the "least," the sinners, the poor.[9]

In Nazareth de Foucauld began to recognize his unfolding vocation, that would lead him ultimately to the deserts of the Sahara to simply live among the Tuareg people, not as a missionary but as a monk. He wrote: "One can be a contemplative, and ought to be, at *all* times— in the midst of words and actions no less than in the silence of the chapel."[10] Little Sister of Jesus Kathleen writes:

> His life wasn't a matter of reconciling prayer and contemplation on the one hand with activities and ministry on the other. He was called to a new form of religious life that drew its inspiration directly from the Incarnation: a contemplative life in the fullest sense of the word, but one that deepened through daily contact with human activity.[11]

Beyond a Balancing Act

In chapter three we considered, in the life of Elijah and the monks who lived near the River Cherith the challenge of living out in a balance the alternating rhythms of rest and activity, between the prophetic and the mystical, between being and doing. We noted that Soelle, for example, speaks of "two worlds": action and contemplation, and of the "return journey" to the world after times of silence and stillness. In the Brook Cherith we saw how Euthymius strived to reconcile the conflicting demands of solitude and hospitality, stability and movement, work and rest—vacillating between alternatives, finding room for each competing need, establishing rhythms and patterns of life permitting a sometimes uncomfortable co-existence between competing elements.

---

9. Kathleen of Jesus, *Universal Brother*, 52.
10. Hamilton, *Desert My Dwelling Place*, 22.
11. Kathleen of Jesus, *Universal Brother*, 67.

But Mary at Nazareth and the Incarnate life of Christ take this further and deeper—not only to achieve some sort of resolution between competing demands but rather, at the very center of their being, to unify and weld together the stillness and action, listening and speaking. Contemplation and action become integrated, part of one another.

As Charles de Foucauld discovered at Nazareth, Jesus models this integration. This is more than an alternating rhythm between withdrawal and engagement, an ebb and flow of prayer and ministry, such as we saw in Elijah. It is rather the bringing of a contemplative heart, a seeing and listening heart, into the very center of work:

> Jesus said to them, "Very truly, I tell you, the Son can do nothing on his own, but only what he sees the Father doing; for whatever the Father does, the Son does likewise. The Father loves the Son and shows him all that he himself is doing . . . As I hear, I judge." (5:19,20,30; see also 14:10)

Mary finds angels both at the well and in the home, angels in the workplace. Can we live in such a way that we entertain angels unawares? The Letter to the Hebrews asks us: "Do not neglect to show hospitality to strangers, for thereby some have entertained angels unawares" (Heb 13:2, RSV). Mary's Well in noisy Nazareth alerts us: rule nothing out. Live with alertness to angels. Even in the midst of action, carry an inner receptive stillness. Become ever more susceptible to the Divine. Develop a greater docility to the Spirit. In the very midst of the demands of work, in the maelstrom of duties and tasks, be ready for the call of God: it will come when you least expect it. Be ready at all times and in all places to echo Mary's *fiat*: "Here I am, the servant of the Lord. Let it be to me according to your word."

QUESTIONS FOR REFLECTION

1. What noise pollution do you have to live with? Name and describe the sounds that fill your ears. How can you hear God in the midst of this?

2. Reflect on the duties and responsibilities you face in daily life. Have you ever "entertained angels unawares" or at least glimpsed the Divine amidst daily chores?

3. Reflect on your last 24 hours. Where did you sense God? Where, perhaps, did you miss God?

4 George Herbert described the experience of prayer as "Heaven in Ordinary" (Prayer 1). See chapter nine for the words of his great hymn "Teach me, my God and King, In all things Thee to see." How can we train ourselves to live out his words: "The one that looks on glass, on it may stay his eye; or if he pleaseth, through it pass, and then the heaven espy" ?

5 How would you sum up De Caussade's teaching? What part of it do you find most challenging? Why?

Dare you use de Foucauld's Prayer of Abandonment? What is holding you back, if anything?

> *Father,*
>
> *I abandon myself into your hands.*
> *Do with me what you will.*
> *Whatever you may do, I thank you;*
> *I am ready for all, I accept all.*
> *Let only your Will be done in me, and in all your creatures.*
> *I wish no more than this, O Lord.*
> *Into your hands I commend my soul.*
> *I offer it to you with all the love of my heart,*
> *for I love you, Lord, and so need to give myself*
> *to surrender myself into your hands*
> *without reserve and with boundless confidence*
> *For you are my Father.*
>
> *Amen.*

Spring at Ein Karem

8

SPRING OF THE VINEYARD, EIN KAREM

Listening With The Heart

In those days Mary set out and went with haste to a Judean town in the hill country, where she entered the house of Zechariah and greeted Elizabeth.
(Luke 1:39)

THE ANCIENT SPRING BUBBLES up at the heart of the picturesque village of Ein Karem, the name meaning "Spring of the Vineyard" or "Generous Spring." Bronze Age pottery has been found nearby. Set at the head of a stunning valley west of Jerusalem, with terraced slopes around as if making an amphitheater, the village has preserved its beautiful natural environment to this day, and its lovely limestone houses have survived the ravages of war. Mary's Spring still flows, gushing out beneath a minaret and mosque long deserted.

In the second Temple period Ein Karem was a Jewish village which welcomed Christian residents when churches celebrating the Visitation of Mary to Elizabath and the birthplace of John the Baptist were built by Byzantines and later by Crusaders. In Ottoman times it flourished as a largely Arab village. In 1883, the Palestine Exploration Fund's *Survey of Western Palestine* described Ein Karem as: "A flourishing village of about 600 inhabitants, 100 being Latin Christians. It stands on a sort of natural terrace projecting from the higher hills on the east of it, with a broad flat valley below on the west. On the south below the village is a fine spring ('Ain Sitti Miriam), with a vaulted place for prayer over it. The water issues from a spout into a trough."[1]

Contemporary Issues

Ein Karem became a place of refuge on 9 April 1948 when residents fleeing the massacre of 110 Arabs at nearby Deir Yassin escaped to the village in the hope of finding safety from their attackers, Zionist paramilitary groups Irgun and Lehi. Their respite was short-lived: on 18 July 1948, as a small part of the 750 thousand Arabs displaced from their homes and fleeing west, the entire Palestinian population of Ein Karem was totally removed and residents became refugees. To this day, one of their potent symbols is the key—for as they fled in the event they call the *Nakba* (Catastrophe), they took the key to their home with them, in the hope of return to the property. But within days the houses were occupied by Jewish immigrants delighting in the newly-declared State of Israel, who have remained put.

So Ein Karem today, for all its natural beauty and charm, raises big issues: not primarily environmental but rather human. The Arab homes of Ein Karem now inhabited by Israelis require us to look at the issue of reconciliation and peace-making. But the tragic fact is that the so-called Peace Process, with its tiny steps towards dialogue and agreement, is in tatters. The gaping chasm between the two sides is growing ever wider. Communication has stalled. Indeed, fragile diplomatic relationships have soured and are marked by deep distrust from both sides. There seems little talking, and practically no listening.

ENCOURAGING ENCOUNTERS

When we turn to the story about Mary and Elizabeth we see that at its heart is trusting encounter. This was no brief visitation. Luke tells us its duration:

> In those days Mary set out and went with haste to a Judean town in the hill country, where she entered the house of Zechariah and greeted Elizabeth. When Elizabeth heard Mary's greeting, the child leapt in her womb. And Elizabeth was filled with the Holy Spirit and exclaimed with a loud cry, "Blessed are you among

---

1. Conder and Kitchener, *Survey of Western Palestine*, 19–21.

women, and blessed is the fruit of your womb. And why has this happened to me, that the mother of my Lord comes to me? For as soon as I heard the sound of your greeting, the child in my womb leapt for joy. And blessed is she who believed that there would be a fulfilment of what was spoken to her by the Lord."

Mary remained with her for about three months and then returned to her home. (Luke 1:39–45,56)

This extended encounter was no superficial meeting: it reached the depths. Like the spring named after her, Mary's heart gushed forth limpid waters of transparent honesty and grace that speak powerfully to us across the centuries as we contemplate our relationships and the quality of our encounters. Four things stand out:

1 Effort in Overcoming Barriers

Mary makes the effort—a long journey to the hill country of Judea—to share with Elizabeth. With determination and a certain sense of urgency Mary undertook a journey of a hundred miles across mountains and valleys, finally reaching the hill county Judea from distant Nazareth. The reference to Mary travelling "with haste" may indicate a state of stress or anxiety. She had to face physical barriers along the way—not only the demanding terrain but also the experience of exhaustion and fatigue. She was pregnant, making the journey even more demanding.

Reaching Elizabeth she had to overcome social barriers. Luke tells us

> In the days of King Herod of Judea, there was a priest named Zechariah, who belonged to the priestly order of Abijah. His wife was a descendant of Aaron, and her name was Elizabeth. Both of them were righteous before God, living blamelessly according to all the commandments and regulations of the Lord. But they had no children, because Elizabeth was barren, and both were getting on in years. (Luke 1:5–7)

Elizabeth and Zechariah were distinguished by belonging to the priestly class and were closely associated with the Temple where Zechariah did duty. Mary, on the other hand, was of peasant stock from a tiny insignificant hamlet and her betrothed was a *tekton*— carpenter, builder or mason, working in wood or stone.

Moreover there was a huge age gap between the women. They belong to different generations. Zechariah says: "I'm an old man and my wife is an old woman" (Luke 1:18, *Message*). The King James Version puts it: they were "well stricken in years." Mary is, as we noted, according to the *Protoevangelium of James*, just sixteen.

The physical and social barriers might have been enough to dissuade Mary from undertaking the journey. She could very easily have stayed in isolation in Nazareth. But she reveals a determination to see the Other, and nothing will stand in her way.

As she arrives in Ein Karem, Zechariah opens the door of his house (Luke 1:40) and welcomes her. He represents those who facilitate such honest exchange between parties, as he literally creates a safe place where deep sharing can take place in an atmosphere of respect. Mute himself at that time, Zechariah powerfully represents those whose key role is to listen—without advising—to the Other.

2 Sharing of Hopes and Fears

For three months Mary and Elizabeth talk and listen to one another. Mary puts into words her experience of the Divine, her encounter with the mysterious angel in the Annunciation and her sense of being called by God—her unfolding vocation. She pours forth her fears, (mentioned both in Luke and *Protoevangelium*). We noted in chapter seven the possible range of Mary's anxieties: a fear of the unknown, a fear of failure or letting God down, a fear of rejection by her own community, a sense perhaps of inadequacy or unworthiness. Such fears were not unfounded: within less than a year Simeon would say to her "A sword will pierce your own soul too." (Luke 2:35).

But she shares also her sense of God's care in her life. Mary sings of her experience of God's providence:

> My soul magnifies the Lord, and my spirit rejoices in God my savior.
> He has looked on the poor degree of his handmaiden.
> Behold, now from henceforth all generations will call me blessed.
> For he who is mighty has done great things unto me, and holy is his name.
> (Luke 1:46–49, NMB)

This is a deep and authentic level of sharing.

Spring Of The Vineyard, Ein Karem

3 Mutual Attentiveness

Elizabeth listens attentively and offers great affirmation: "Blessed are you among women . . . Blessed is she who believed." In these words Elizabeth displays an attitude of respect and reverence towards the Other. She honors Mary's dignity. She salutes Mary's God-bearing. She responds to Mary's youthful vulnerability with strong encouragement. Elizabeth herself is vulnerable, being pregnant as an elderly woman, facing uncertainties and worries. She too has questions and is trying to make sense of things, asking: "why has this happened to me?" Here is a profound communication between the two women, represented by the babies in the wombs greeting each other and leaping or dancing within. This extended conversation is marked by questions and affirmations, by laughter and tears. It is an encounter and depth of meeting enabled both by human openness and transparency given by the Holy Spirit (1:42). It is a gracious and courageous encounter brimming with honesty, integrity, emotion and trust.

4 Alertness to Justice

Mary goes on to share with Elizabeth her hopes and in the praises of the Magnificat declares her faith in One who turns things upside down, seeks justice for the marginalized, oppressed and down-trodden:

> His mercy is on them who fear him, throughout all generations.
> He scatters those who are proud in the imagination of their hearts.
> He puts down the mighty from their seats and exalts those of low degree.
> He fills the hungry with good things and sends the rich away empty.
> (Luke 1:50–53, NMB)

Gebara and Bingemar observe:

> Deep down [in the Magnificat] there is the experience of the ever-renewed possibility of hope, the never-ending desire for justice, the ever-renewed yearning for a love that can satisfy the eternal yearning to love. "His mercy is from age to age on those who fear him" (1:50). Each generation takes up this ceaseless quest, and leaves as a legacy the insatiable yearnings for love, mercy, justice . . .[2]

---

2. Gebara and Bingemar, *Mother of the Poor*, 72.

Mary's conversation with Elizabeth, then, does not only focus on her particular vocation: from it issues an urgent and heartfelt cry for justice between all peoples. This extended time of listening and sharing pours forth an impassioned confidence in the God who turns things upside down and inside out, for the Magnificat is, above all, a declaration of faith in the one who "scatters the proud in the imagination of their hearts / pulls down the mighty from their seats / and exalts the humble and meek" (*Book of Common Prayer*).

Two major themes emerge from this joyful mystery.

1 LEARNING THE ART OF CONTEMPLATIVE LISTENING

Mary and Elizabeth stand as models of the practice of contemplative listening. Meaningful interaction with others entails attentive listening to the Other. Listening requires a focused attentiveness to the Other.

A double listening is required before any speaking: a listening to God and a discovery of the hopes and hurts in our community.

First we learn to listen inwardly...

- to our own heart, our feelings and responses to God
- to the inner word of God: God's whispers and intimations
- to the word of God in Scripture to us

But we also learn to listen to what God is saying to us outwardly in

- the cries of the poor
- the screams of the oppressed
- the sobs of the broken-hearted
- the sighs of our culture
- the laughter in people's lives
- in those around us—both what is said, and what is left unsaid
- the shrieks of the young and the groans of the elderly

It is difficult to discern the voice of God, but we need to learn to listen to what "the Spirit is saying to the churches" and to read the "signs of the times." Richard Foster encourages us to: "meditate upon the events of our time and to seek to penetrate their significance. We have a spiritual obligation to penetrate the inner meaning of events and political pressures, not to gain power, but to gain prophetic perspective."[3] As we develop the practice of such discipline, we discover where people are hurting, and where human dignity is being eroded. We echo Isaiah's comment: "The Lord God has opened my ear" (Isa 50:5). The Scripture is emphatic: "O that today you would listen to his voice!" (Ps 95:7).

Sometimes God speaks to us through unexpected means. C.S. Lewis put it powerfully:

> God whispers to us in our pleasures, speaks to us in our conscience, but shouts to us in our pains: it is his megaphone to rouse a deaf world . . . No doubt Pain as God's megaphone is a terrible instrument... But it gives the only opportunity the bad man can have for amendment. It removes the veil; it plants the flag of truth within the fortress of a rebel soul.[4]

Lewis suggests that the experience of pain can shatter the illusion that all is well with us, destroying the false idea that we can get very nicely by without God. Pain shatters the illusion of self-sufficiency, for it causes us to reach out to God either in petition or complaint. It makes us wake up to the big questions of God and evil, and can draw us into a new surrender to God, the communion for which we were created. Suffering does indeed has a revelatory character, for those with eyes to see it. God speaks most powerfully through the experience of poverty and pain, calling us to simplicity and trust.

Using the Ears of Your Heart

In the Christian tradition, the call to listen is frequent. The *Rule of St Benedict* opens with the imperative "listen!" and then goes on: "listen with the ear of your heart." This is a deep and contemplative sort of listening. As the Book of Common Prayer's intercessions put it, may the congregation both "hear and receive thy holy word." It is a receptive, not-judging listening that we're called to—the sort that is able to suspend judgment and lets go of imposing our own agendas and solutions. This is a listening that is utterly open, open to surprises, and unshockable!

---

3. Foster, *Celebration of Discipline*, 28.
4. Lewis, *Problem of Pain*, 81, 83.

The Quaker Douglas Steere puts it: "To listen another's soul into a condition of disclosure and discovery may be almost the greatest service that any human being ever performs for another."[5] The listening which we must practice requires then, a readiness to move, literally and metaphorically, towards the Other. It requires our undivided awareness and undistracted attention. It is intentionally focused on the Other. It must remain open-ended in the sense that it is not directed toward an outcome. It builds trust and enables true dialogue in which we suspend personal opinion and judgment. We listen in order to discover what we might learn from worlds outside our own. We hone our skills in beginning to see things from another's perspective. In learning to listen with attentiveness to others we start to listen to God.

2 FORGING SPIRITUAL FRIENDSHIPS

Mary and Elizabeth, standing by the gushing Spring of the Vineyard at Ein Karem would urge us to go further, and explore the idea and practice of spiritual friendship.

These days, the word "friends" often gets devalued. Aside from the excellent comedy by that name, (which might give us useful clues about friendship), we see the term used on social media—where such a relationship might be "a mile wide and an inch deep." But as pilgrims on a journey, we need spiritual friends who can support us and cheer us on our way, and to whom we can offer such encouragement. Throughout the Scriptures we find inspiring examples of how spiritual friendships transform and deepen our life in God. Who can you recall?

Remember, for example, the remarkable friendship and depth of sharing between David and Jonathan, Jesus with John the beloved disciple, Mary, Martha and Lazarus; Peter and Mark; Paul and Timothy. Throughout the history of the Church examples abound: Gregory Nazianzen and Basil; Jerome and Paula; Augustine and Monica; Benedict and Scholastica, Francis and Clare; Bernard of Clairvaux and his brother; Teresa of Avila and John of the Cross; Jane of Chantal and Francis de Sales . . . so why not us, in our day?

---

5. Steere, *On Listening to Another*. See also Long, *Listening*; Hedahl, *Listening Ministry*; Justes, *Hearing Beyond Words*.

Spring Of The Vineyard, Ein Karem

What Does Scripture Say of Such Friendships?

Faithful friends are a sturdy shelter:
   whoever finds one has found a treasure.
Faithful friends are beyond price;
   no amount can balance their worth.
Faithful friends are life-saving medicine;
   those who fear the Lord will find them.
Those who fear the Lord direct their friendship aright,
   for as they are, so are their neighbors also. (Eccl 6:14–17)

A friend loves at all times. (Prov 17:17)

How wonderful and pleasant it is
   when brothers and sisters live together in harmony!
For harmony is as precious as the anointing oil
    that was poured over Aaron's head,
    that ran down his beard and onto the border of his robe.
Harmony is as refreshing as the dew from Mount Hermon
   that falls on the mountains of Zion.
And there the Lord has pronounced his blessing,
   even life everlasting. (Ps 133, NLT)

Where two or three are gathered in my name, I am there among them. (Matt 18:20)

I do not call you servants any longer, because the servant does not know what the master is doing; but I have called you friends, because I have made known to you everything that I have heard from my Father. (John 15:15)

Share each other's burdens, and in this way obey the law of Christ. (Gal 6:2 NLT)

If then there is any encouragement in Christ, any consolation from love, any sharing in the Spirit, any compassion and sympathy, make my joy complete: be of the same mind, having the same love, being in full accord and of one mind. Do nothing from selfish ambition or conceit, but in humility regard others as better than yourselves. Let each of you look not to your own interests, but to the interests of others. Let the same mind be in you that was in Christ Jesus . . . (Phil 2:1–5)

The Need

In our own lives of faith, people often live at some distance from one other. There can be both physical loneliness and also a sense of spiritual isolation. We wonder to ourselves—"am I the only one struggling spiritually with this?" Or, "that was such a blessing, I wish I had someone to share it with!" Learning the art of spiritual friendship might be the precursor to a fuller experience of spiritual direction...

Spiritual Friendship: What It Can Be

Regular two-way attentive conversation focusing on the life of faith and the experience of prayer can be a tool to develop thoughtful refection on context and how that shapes our life of prayer. It makes possible a celebration of everyday spirituality and how that shapes our work, relationships, witness. The two become companions on the spiritual journey. As a regular discipline in which one shares with a friend aspects of one's relationship with God, it attends to both the ways we pray and how that affects our daily living. It should be reciprocal and mutual—a 50/50 relationship in terms of time and attentiveness.

Careful contemplative listening to another's soul can help them to discern God by asking sensitive questions which prompt the person to clarify, recognize, notice and name, and pick up clues about God's presence in their life. This develops greater awareness of God and gently encourages greater openness to God. It involves asking questions, not giving answers: going beneath the superficial "how are you?" to "how is your soul? How is your relationship with God right now? What is holding you back from...? What is helping you most...?" It requires a sense of mutual accountability under God. It is absolutely confidential. It is characterized by a non-judgmental acceptance of the Other. Listening to one another requires a measure of self-restraint and holding-back from advice-giving, our default mode! It requires a discipline of listening and keeping boundaries, such as time-keeping, with a clear beginning and ending to each session. It can be considered as an everyday expression of spiritual direction. Above all, the relationship is marked by equality, reciprocity, honesty and total trust. It will prove to be a source of re-assurance and, from time-to-time, of challenge.

Spiritual friendship is to be clearly distinguished from counselling, confession, mentoring or coaching. It is not correcting or judging ("if I were you"). It is not problem-centered but growth-centered. It should not stray into commenting on church life / church politics or other people in the church community or evaluating sermons! It is about the soul.

Spiritual friendship is fostered and maintained by an informal covenant or agreement between the two parties. They need to agree time and place and duration (for example, 30 minutes each, once a fortnight in Lent; other times, monthly?). The two should clarify goals, asking: why are we doing this, what is the aim? How frequently shall we meet? Where shall we meet? For how long will we meet? The actual practice of the conversation will involve the two participants alternating roles—from speaker to listener, and vice versa. This is a spiritual conversation but with emphasis on the listener clarifying, feeding back, summarizing. It might conclude by agreeing an action point: what prayer practice shall we experiment with or commit to this time ?

In such a spiritual conversation, it is best to use open questions, inviting reflection—not closed questions requiring a yes/no answer! The aim is not gathering information. The aim is being "in formation," encouraging a sense of progress sometimes (not always!). The aim is helping the Other come to a greater clarity about their relationship with God and enabling them (not you) identify possible steps forward . . . These kind of questions might be helpful:

- What is impacting your life of prayer from your context?
- What factors around you exert influences on your prayer life?
- What type of influences do they exert?
- How has the last month been for you, spiritually speaking?
- What has good been for you this last week, in your relationship with God?
- Where did you feel closest to God?
- Where did you feel most distant?
- How do you recognize the presence of God in your life, what clues or indicators are you looking for?
- What are the signs that the Holy Spirit is working in you?
- In what ways are you growing spiritually?
- In what ways do you want to grow, and take steps forward?

- How have you been praying? (referring to prayer practices)
- What is your experience of silence?
- What is your experience of listening to God?
- What is your heart's desire, in relation to God?

The Fruits of Contemplative Listening

As we become more articulate in speaking of matters of the spirit, of the inner life, of our relationship with God—this will equip us to be more confident witnesses (even evangelists) as we become better able to put into words what is going on in the soul.[6] The practice of contemplative listening will equip us for our daily ministry of being alongside people and supporting people. It enables new and deeper friendships to develop in church community—with less superficiality, richer relationships and deeper fellowship in the congregation. This can be for everyone, not just the "holy few"—and will no doubt add to the health and well-being of the whole congregation. Perhaps the experience might suggest an evolving vocation—to some form of ministry, perhaps to be trained as spiritual director? Greater awareness and alertness to the movements of the Holy Spirit in us, with the help of a trusted friend, will lead to greater clarity about our calling.

VOICES FROM THE SPRING

Salesian Insights

One group of Christians who have long pondered the significance of the Visitation event are those who belong to the Order of the Visitation, founded in 1610 by **Francis de Sales** (1567–1622) and **Jane Frances de Chantal** (1572–1641) in Annecy, France. At first, Francis did not have a religious order in mind: he wished to form a congregation, where the enclosed cloister need be observed only during the year of novitiate, after which the sisters should be free to go out by turns to visit the sick and poor. The Order was given the name of The Visitation with the intention that the sisters would follow the example of Virgin Mary and her joyful visit to Elizabeth. The special charism of the Visitation Order is the practice of two

---

6. On learning the vocabulary of faith see Mayes, *Language of the Soul*.

virtues, humility and gentleness, overflowing like a spring into a stream of unselfconscious care:

> Salesian Spirituality is optimism. It's gentleness. It's strength. It's blooming where you're planted and living in the present moment. It's ordinary acts done in an extraordinary way. It's living in the presence of God in whatever you do, be it in prayer, in class, or in the workplace. These are some of the virtues that Salesian Spirituality celebrates.[7]

Echoing the foundational story of Mary's visitation to her cousin, Francis de Sales has much to teach us about forging open, listening relationships. He writes in his *Introduction to the Devout Life*:

> Travel with a good guide ... Trust God, who will speak to you and grant graces through that person. God will put into their heart and on their lips whatever is necessary for your happiness ... Open your heart to them truthfully and sincerely, tell them everything good and bad, hide nothing and pretend nothing ... let your relationship be strong, sacred, entirely spiritual and divine ... Pray to find such a person and bless God when you find them; then remain constant and seek no further but go forward in simplicity, humility and confidence, for your journey will be attended with every success.[8]
>
> What a wonderful thing it is to love on earth as we shall love in heaven, to cherish one another in this world as we shall forever in the next. When I speak of charity here, I am not referring to the love we should have for everyone, but to a spiritual friendship by which two or more people share their devotion and aspirations with each other, and become one in spirit.[9]

We Need The Holy Spirit

Reflecting on the events of Ein Karem, Salesian Sister Susan Marie highlights the need for the divine Spirit to facilitate and animate deep sharing:

> By entering the Visitation mystery, by focusing on the Holy Spirit's powerful engagement in the Visitation narrative, we can ask the Spirit to act and move among us in a similar way to the Spirit's

---

7. Ogden, "Optimism of Salesian Spirituality."
8. de Sales, *Devout Life*, 13.
9. de Sales, *Devout Life*, 139.

action between Mary and Elizabeth, also reflected between the unborn infants Jesus and John.

The Holy Spirit's power pervaded all aspects of the encounter between Mary and Elizabeth. When Mary arrived in the town of Judah, entered the house and greeted Elizabeth, Elizabeth "heard" Mary's greeting. She *listened*. Listening, a simple yet intense action is the receptivity needed in order to be grasped by the Spirit. The Gospel states quite distinctly that Elizabeth "was filled" with the Holy Spirit. Spiritual gifts then flowed out in abundance. She became a witness with a prophetic voice. She began to proclaim the truth about the present moment; deep, essential truths.

Elizabeth proclaimed, loudly, "Blest are you among women and blest is the fruit of your womb." Her initial truth was a statement about Mary's *identity*, as a blessed one. "But who am I that the Mother of my Lord should come to me?" The gift of *humility* is so clearly expressed here.

Elizabeth's proclamation also revealed the gift of knowledge given to her. She knew Mary's condition, that she was expecting a Child, she knew that the unborn child is Lord, her Lord. We too can ask for the gift of *knowledge*; it is a gift given within the Gospel event of the Visitation.

The power of the Holy Spirit within us helps us see and proclaim the truth of our circumstances, our path, and our relationship with the Lord, as each continues to say, "but who am I?"

"Blessed is she who trusted that the Lord's words to her would be fulfilled."

Trust. We really need to trust and to deepen it. We have received the individual promise of our God to our hearts. We are called to trust that the promises God has made to us will be fulfilled.[10]

Speak and Listen—From the Heart

There are glimpses of light amidst the shadows of the present breakdown in the Peace Process of which Ein Karem reminds us. There are people and groups that are prepared to listen to one another without prejudgment. I have been privileged to facilitate an interfaith sharing group under the auspices of the Episcopal Diocese of Jerusalem. It brought together small number of Jews, Muslims and Christians so that they could share their

---

10. Sister Susan Marie "Visitation Sisters' Charism and the Holy Spirit."

experience and reflect on it. It had a golden rule, established and agreed when the group was first formed: people must only speak from the heart, and listen from the heart. That, indeed, seems to sum up the challenge and invitation of Mary and Elizabeth beside the Spring of the Vineyard.[11]

QUESTIONS FOR REFLECTION

1. What situations are you aware of—both in your situation and in the wider world—where communication has broken down, and where people seem not to be listening to one another?
2. Is there any part you can play in encouraging communication in your setting?
3. Are you a good listener? How would you know?
4. Is there anyone in your spiritual community to whom you could offer a listening ear—and heart?
5. What is your experience of "spiritual friendship" or of spiritual direction—both giving and receiving it? How can you widen and deepen this?

---

11. See Mayes, *Gateways to the Divine*.

Pilgrim at Jacob's Well

9

JACOB'S WELL, SAMARIA

Transforming Perception

*Jesus left Judea and started back to Galilee.
But he had to go through Samaria. (John 4:3,4)*

Why did Jesus *have* to go through the hated land of Samaria? What made it imperative to take the route northwards between Mount Ebal and Mount Gerizim in the Samaritan highlands, past Jacob's Well?

In order to make a journey from Jerusalem to Galilee, Jesus had in fact the choice of three routes. The Via Maris, the magnificent Roman Road that followed the coastal plain, thrived as the main trade route from Egypt to Mesopotamia. This was an undemanding road, favored by traders and merchants.

A second route followed the Jordan Valley. There one could walk in the great rift valley within sight of the River itself.

A third route was tricky and unpopular, for it traversed Samaritan territory. It was difficult in places, because these are the central highlands of the country, with steeply-sided hills and meandering ravines. Indeed, a valley south of Shechem is called, to this day, the Valley of the Thieves, because historically it was a place of ambush and attack. But of course this third route was undesirable from a Jewish point of view, because, as John reminds us, "Jews have no dealings with Samaritans." In Jewish eyes,

Samaritans were hated pariahs, half-castes, religiously impure and to take this route would defile and contaminate the Jewish traveler. They were a despised underclass, a bastard people. Ever since the Assyrian deportation of the population in 722BC and the subsequent repopulating of the area with people of different bloods, Jews looked upon Samaritans with disdain. Samaria had become a hostile, no-go area. However, John tells us: "he left Judea and started back to Galilee. But he *had* to go through Samaria" (John 4:3,4). So why?

What divine imperative impelled Jesus to choose this most treacherous way? It is vital for Jesus to take this route, it is necessary for one reason alone: Jesus had an inner compulsion wanting the disciples to travel through liminal terrain where they would be profoundly changed. Jesus was insistent on this passage to Galilee because he wanted his disciples to enter marginal, despised territory where many of their most cherished ideas about God and humanity would be shattered and reconstructed. For Jesus, there was simply no other way! It turns out to be a transitional route in more than one sense. There will be the outer journey taking place, but an inner journey too—unsettling shifts in perception. In John's perspective, Jesus takes his disciples to Samaria for no less a reason than to expose them to radical paradigm shifts, to lead them to a breakthrough in attitudes. He takes them to Jacob's Well to help the disciples transcend traditional categories of thought. He wants to liberate them from the straitjackets and prisons of inherited prejudice and stereotyping.

JACOB'S WELL THEN

The Well lies at the center of the story in John 4.

> So he came to a Samaritan city called Sychar, near the plot of ground that Jacob had given to his son Joseph. Jacob's well was there, and Jesus, tired out by his journey, was sitting by the well. It was about noon. (John 4:5–6)

> [The Samaritan woman said:] "The well is deep . . . Are you greater than our ancestor Jacob, who gave us the well, and with his sons and his flocks drank from it?" (John 4:11,12)

In fact, this ancient well turns out to encapsulate the very vocation of the Woman, and to become a symbol of her potential: the Woman will become a well for others, for Jesus looks at her and promises: "the water that I will give you will become in you a well of water springing up to eternal life" (WEB). This well will become, indeed, the very symbol of the human calling. Outcast, derided and ostracized by her community for her unusually wide experience of the opposite sex ("you have had five husbands, and the one you have now is not your husband," John 4:18), she is forced to draw water at the height of the noonday sun when the well would be deserted. Her low esteem, her experience of rejection is overcome by Jesus' gracious and healing affirmation: "You are worthy to bear the divine Water of the Spirit!"

JACOB'S WELL TODAY

Today Jacob's Well is protected by a magnificent church. Earlier Byzantine and Crusader constructions have long been destroyed by earthquake or violence, and the site was in a ruinous state when I first visited it in October 1979, though the foundations of a new building were in place. Jacob's Well has also been a site of contention and violence. In 1979 a Zionist group claimed it as a Jewish holy place and demanded that crosses and icons be removed. A week later the custodian, Archimandrite Philoumenos Kassapis, was butchered to death by 35 axe-strokes in the crypt and the church was desecrated. No one was ever convicted of his murder. He was declared a martyr by the Orthodox church and his tomb has become a shrine in the upper church: in the intervening decades a noble Orthodox church has been raised, with the ancient well preserved in the crypt.

Just 200 yards or a 3 minute walk from the church is a place pilgrims do not visit: the appallingly overcrowded refugee camp of Balata. As I write, many Palestinians have been killed in the vicinity by Israeli troops. But the recent tensions and heartache of the site go back to 1950 when, in the aftermath of the Israeli War of Independence, a refugee camp was begun nearby. In 1950 it was designed to offer temporary shelter to 5000 Palestinians fleeing their villages to the west. Today it has become the largest camp in the West Bank, 30 thousand people crammed into a site measuring one square kilometer. Its narrow lanes and tight alleys squeeze their way between tenement buildings rudely constructed where tents and shacks had stood. Perpetually in shadow of Mount Ebal it is marked by unemployment and depression, fueling the despair of armed resistance groups.¹ The UN reports: "Life in the camp is intensified by weekly search and arrest operations conducted by Israeli Security Forces (ISF). These often occur at night, resulting in damage to residents' homes and a sense of fear and anxiety, especially among young children."² Since 1967 many Jewish settlements have been erected in the environs of this part of the occupied West Bank, exacerbating intense conflict.

Like the Woman at the Well, the residents of Balata feel demoralized, forgotten and without a future. Like her they have descended into a pessimistic mindset. Outsiders, too, can see only gloom. The *Times of Israel* reports:

> The largest and one of most notorious of the camps . . . Balata sits only a few kilometers from the heart of Nablus. Over decades, the residents here have developed a unique, separate sense of identity — as the most disadvantaged and oppressed members of Palestinian society.³

The *Washington Post* calls Balata "the city of Nablus's roughest refugee camp."⁴

LEARNING FROM BIBLICAL SHECHEM

Before we turn again to John 4 to see how Jesus revolutionizes perception and our way of seeing things, we recall the backstory—for it was precisely at the site of Jacob's Well and Balata that the Patriarchs of old made significant decisions in their outlooks. This, indeed is ancient Shechem: the ancient ruins of the city are to be found next door to Jacob's Well at Tel Balata.

1 Abraham: Be Ready to Move Forward

The Letter to Hebrews celebrates Abraham as the archetypal pilgrim:

> By faith Abraham obeyed when he was called to set out for a place that he was to receive as an inheritance; and by faith he stayed for a time in the land he had been promised, as in a foreign land, living

---

1. Murphy gives an account of her living for 3 months in Balata camp in *Between River and Sea*.
2. UNRWA, "Profile: Balata Camp."
3. Issacharoff, "Refugee Camp."
4. Berger, Booth and AbdulKarim, "A new generation."

in tents. For he looked forward to the city that has foundations, whose architect and builder is God. (Heb 11:8–10)

Genesis relates his journey:

> Now the Lord said to Abram, "Go from your country and your kindred and your father's house to the land that I will show you." . . . When they had come to the land of Canaan, Abram passed through the land to the place at Shechem, to the oak of Moreh. At that time the Canaanites were in the land. Then the Lord appeared to Abram, and said, "To your offspring I will give this land." So he built there an altar to the Lord, who had appeared to him. (Gen 12:1, 6–9)

God commands: "Go from your country." He was prepared to quit his comfort zone, leave behind his home, and venture forth on a journey into the unknown. He was prepared to let go of his familiar securities, even his cherished inherited concepts of God, and move out on a journey of faith: "he set out, not knowing where he was going" (Heb 11). Abraham truly had a pilgrim heart. He was prepared to live with vulnerability and risk, quitting his comfortable stone house, ready to be "living in tents" (Heb 11:9).

We too find ourselves on a spiritual journey and we must keep moving. We have not arrived. We must be prepared, like Abraham himself, to let go sometimes of conventions and concepts that would pull us back and tie us down. We must be prepared, as it were, to "live in tents"—to live with the provisional, the impermanent, the uncomfortable, the unsettling, for as long as it takes. We do not know the outcome of our journey, but God does. God calls us to keep moving forwards. Let us pray for the faith of Abraham to grow in our own hearts, an unshakable trust in God, the God of our journey. Paul puts it: "you are Abraham's offspring, heirs according to the promise" (Gal 3: 28).

2 Jacob: Let Go Of Idols

Throughout the story of the Israelites they are plagued by the temptation to idolatry. It is something that will not go away. Jacob attempts to deal decisively with this at Shechem:

> Jacob said to his household and to all who were with him, "Put away the foreign gods that are among you, and purify yourselves, and change your clothes . . . So they gave to Jacob all the foreign

> gods that they had, and the rings that were in their ears; and Jacob hid them under the oak that was near Shechem. (Gen 35:1–4)

Shechem now becomes a place where wooden and metal idols would be interred, and other trinkets associated with the cult of idolatry. The very place of Abraham's decisive break with the past now is a place for letting go of attachments that have become fruitless and soul-destroying.

3 Joshua: Choose the Good

Joshua, who had led the Israelites into the promised land in succession to Moses, has one great act to complete before he dies. He wants to give his people the opportunity to decisively renew their commitment to God and make an act of rededication. As Deuteronomy tells its story, this was somehow anticipated by Moses himself:

> See, I am setting before you today a blessing and a curse: the blessing, if you obey the commandments of the Lord your God that I am commanding you today; and the curse, if you do not obey the commandments of the Lord your God, but turn from the way that I am commanding you today, to follow other gods that you have not known. When the Lord your God has brought you into the land that you are entering to occupy, you shall set the blessing on Mount Gerizim and the curse on Mount Ebal. (Deut 11:26–29)

And so the time comes for this great act of renewal at Shechem:

> Then Joshua gathered all the tribes of Israel to Shechem, and summoned the elders, the heads, the judges, and the officers of Israel; and they presented themselves before God. And Joshua said to all the people . . . "Choose this day whom you will serve, whether the gods your ancestors served in the region beyond the River or the gods of the Amorites in whose land you are living; but as for me and my household, we will serve the Lord." . . .
> The people said to Joshua, "The Lord our God we will serve, and him we will obey." So Joshua made a covenant with the people that day, and made statutes and ordinances for them at Shechem. Joshua wrote these words in the book of the law of God; and he took a large stone, and set it up there in the sanctuary of the Lord. Joshua said to all the people, "See, this stone shall be a witness against us; for it has heard all the words of the Lord that he spoke to us; therefore it shall be a witness against you, if you deal falsely with your God." So Joshua sent the people away to their inheritances. (Josh 24:1,15–18, 24–28)

It is still possible to stand of this very spot today in the West Bank outside Nablus at the site of the ancient city of Shechem located in the valley midway between mounts Ebal and Gerizim. Archeology has revealed at Tel Balata the walls of the temple of Baal-berith—the temple of the Lord of the covenant. Indeed a stone akin to Joshua's great monolith has been set up by this sanctuary. Poignantly, this site is close by Jacob's Well of John 4 which centuries later would come to witness a call to see things differently.

The accounts of Abraham, Jacob and Joshua at Shechem speak of a willingness to let go of the past and to let go of negative or destructive thinking, symbolized by Abraham's readiness to move forward, and represented in the idols interred here by Jacob and in the decisiveness to break from the past that Joshua engendered in his people.

As we return to John 4's account of Jesus at Jacob's Well we see these as foretastes of the radical call to re-thinking that Jesus offers.

JESUS AT JACOB'S WELL
Dare to See Things Differently

While in Samaria, Jesus encounters people with a fixation with surface, superficial and crassly material ways of viewing things and leads his hearers into a radically different way of looking at the world.

First it is the Woman that Jesus wants to lead into a different approach to perception. Twice over the Woman is stuck on a literal and physical hearing of Jesus' words about water: "Sir, you have no bucket, and the well is deep. Where do you get that living water? . . . Sir, give me this water, so that I may never be thirsty or have to keep coming here to draw water" (4:11, 15). But Jesus wants to lead her from the physicality of the water to its sacramentality, and how it powerfully symbolizes the gift of God. The physical water, and the well speak to Jesus of humanity's deep thirst for things of the Spirit and God's gracious provision. As the twelfth century Armenian poet puts it:

> O Fountain of life, you asked for water from the woman of Samaria,
> And promised her living water, in return for the transitory one.
> Grant to me, O Fountain of Life, That holy drink for my soul,
> That flows from the heart in rivers,
> The Spirit from whom grace gushes forth.[5]

---

5. Kudian, *Nerses Shnorhali*, 45.

Second, the disciples too are utterly bewitched by a concern for physical things. They had gone into the town to buy food (4:8). Upon their return, they urge him, "Rabbi, eat something" (4:31). 'But he said to them, "I have food to eat that you do not know about." So the disciples said to one another, "Surely no one has brought him something to eat?"'(4:32,33).

Jesus sees food as highly symbolic and sacramental. In chapter six John will put on the lips of Jesus: "the bread that I will give for the life of the world is my flesh" (6:51). There, he will be misunderstood, and be accused of advocating cannibalism. Another response will be to ask for a continual supply of free, fresh bread (6:34). His hearers stay on the level of the physical and cannot glimpse sacramentality. In Samaria he explains: "My food is to do the will of him who sent me" (4:34). He is not talking about a picnic brought to him. He is talking of the deep nourishment and sustenance that comes from moving within the Father's will.

This sacramental way of viewing reality is a dominant theme in the fourth gospel. Jesus sees wine, vines, water, bread, sunlight and candlelight, even shepherding as speaking of himself. The other gospels combine to give us the clear impression that this was an outlook on the world that was truly characteristic of Jesus himself. The secrets of the Kingdom reveal themselves through parables of seed, mountain, field and sea (Matt 13, Mark 11:23). Jesus says: "Consider the lilies, how they grow..." (Luke 12:27). "Consider": the Greek word means "turn your attention to this, notice what is happening, take note." It is a summons to a contemplative way of life, a deeply reflective way of seeing the world. It stands in utter contrast with the way the Woman and the disciples see things—they can't see past a bucket of water or a plate of food! "Take a look around you" Jesus says to the disciples. Learn to see things differently...

NAME AND RECOGNIZE HIDDEN POTENTIAL

At Jacob's Well Jesus shows how it is possible to open our eyes to potential and possibilities hiding in plain sight. He helps people glimpse opportunities instead of seeing dead-ends.

1 Jesus sees the Woman not as an Outcast but as a Well of Living Water

First, as we noticed, Jesus transforms the life of the Woman by helping her see things differently. He celebrates her potential: "The water I give will become in you a spring of water gushing up to eternal life" (John 4:14). She moves from being outcast to evangelist, from reject to ambassador. Demoralization shifts to self-confidence as she accepts that she need not see herself as a used / abused victim but rather as a strong clear witness to divine possibilities. She turns from self-pity or a feeling of worthlessness to courage and boldness: 'Then the woman left her water-jar and went back to the city. She said to the people, "Come and see a man who told me everything I have ever done! He cannot be the Messiah, can he?"' (John 4:28,29)

2 Jesus sees the Harvest not as Distant but as Present

Jesus wants to open the disciples to a new vision and a fresh way of seeing reality.

> Don't you say, "There are still four more months, then comes the harvest"? Listen to what I'm telling you: Open your eyes and look at the fields, for they are ready for harvest. (HCSB)

He calls them to lift up their eyes: "Look around you, and see how the fields are already ripe for harvesting." In the Samarian fields, all that the disciples can see is the first hints of growth, the early shoot from the seed. They expect to have to wait four long months to see a crop ready for harvesting. But Jesus sees things differently. As he looks at the green shoots he sees the full bloom of the plant, and moreover, he sees this as God speaking to him that the *kairos*, the time of opportunity, is here, right now! Indeed, Jesus can recognize his glorification and resurrection is such a seed. Jesus looks at a seed and sees its potential: "unless a grain of wheat falls into the earth and dies, it remains just a single grain; but if it dies, it bears much fruit" (12:24). He glimpses his very destiny in a kernel of wheat.

This is how Jesus wants us to see things. With him, we can see in a pinch of yeast a batch of fresh loaves (Matt 13:33). We can glimpse a tree spreading its branches to welcome the birds of the air—in a tiny mustard seed (Matt 13:31). Where other people look on the surface, or see only limitations, Jesus sees deep possibilities. He rejects an outlook of fatalism or resignation. As he gazes on the motley band of fragile disciples he says, with confidence, and maybe with a smile: "See, the kingdom of God is within you!" (Luke 17:21, NOG)

VOICES FROM THE SPRING

Spirituality of Seeing

Prayer enables an awakening of the spirit and the body: a coming fully-alive, aware and responsive to what God wants to offer us. In prayer we seek fresh vision, wider perspective. Of course, we can also be blinkered and suffer from spiritual myopia. **Ephrem** (d.373), the prolific and inspiring Syriac writer, encourages us in prayer to see reality differently, using his famed image of the "luminous eye" which can look into the hiddenness of God's mystery:

> Blessed is the person who has acquired a luminous eye
> with which he will see how much the angels stand in awe of You, Lord,
> and how audacious is man.[6]

Ephrem encourages us to pray for the gift of the inner eye, which penetrates the deep things of God and gives true in-sight. In this way our prayer can become luminous, radiant and light-revealing:

> Let our prayer be a mirror, Lord, placed before Your face;
> Then Your fair beauty will be imprinted on its luminous surface...[7]

Ephrem reveals an astonishing sacramental world-view, in which all of the created order brims with the Divine and teaches us about God's ways. This is not a utilitarian approach to the natural world, looking around for helpful illustrations or analogies for the spiritual life. Rather, it is a question of training ourselves to recognize the revelatory character of creation and how God teaches us through it:

> In every place, if you look, His symbol is there...
> Lord, Your symbols are everywhere
> Blessed is the Hidden One shining out.[8]

---

6. "Hymn on Faith 3," Brock, *Luminous Eye*, 73.
7. "Hymn on the Church 29," Brock, *Luminous Eye*, 75.
8. "Hymn on the Nativity 21" and "Hymn on Faith 4," *Luminous Eye*, 39.

The Third Eye

Christian philosophers in 12th century Paris, at the monastery of St Victor, literally open our eyes to new ways of seeing, fresh approaches to perception.

First, **Hugh of St. Victor** (1096–1141) distinguished between *cogitatio*, *meditatio*, and *contemplatio*. *Cogitatio*, or simple empirical cognition, is a seeking for the facts of the material world using the eye of flesh. *Meditatio* is a seeking for the truths within oneself (the *imago* of God) using the mind's eye. *Contemplatio* is the knowledge gained by transcendent insight, revealed by the eye of contemplation. **Richard of St. Victor** (1110–1173) affirmed that each level of sight and insight, represented in the three eyes, builds on the previous one.[9] We begin with utilizing the first eye, the eye of flesh, through the senses. We progress by employing a second eye through meditation or reflection. But deepest vision is attained by the third eye—the inner eye—giving us glimpses of true understanding through contemplation. Rohr explains:

> Third-eye seeing is the way mystics see. They do not reject the first eye; the senses matter to them. Nor do they reject the second eye; but they know not to confuse knowledge with depth or mere correct information with the transformation of consciousness itself. The mystical gaze builds upon the first two eyes—and yet goes further. It happens whenever, by some wondrous "coincidence," our heart space, our mind space, and our body awareness are all simultaneously open and nonresistant . . . I like to call it *presence*. It is experienced as a moment of deep inner connection, and it always pulls you, intensely satisfied, into the naked and undefended now, which can include both profound joy and profound sadness at the same time. At that point, you either want to write poetry, pray, or be utterly silent.[10]

In the next century, Eckhart (1260–1328) calls us to a high state of wakefulness, watchfulness and mindfulness, if we are to see God in this life:

> In all our acts and in all things we should consciously use our reason, having in all things a perceptive awareness of ourselves and our inward being, and in all things seize God...For indeed, people who are expectant like that are watchful, they look around them to

---

9. Richard of St. Victor, *De Sacramentis*.
10. Rohr, *Naked Now*, 28.

see where God whom they expect is coming from...This requires much diligence, demanding a total effort of our senses and powers of mind.[11]

Catherine of Sienna summons us: "Look into the depth...of divine charity. For unless you see you cannot love. The more you see, the more you can love."[12] Francis de Sales called contemplation "a loving, simple and permanent attentiveness of the mind to divine things."[13] The *Catechism of the Catholic Church* calls it "a gaze of faith," "a silent love."[14] A story from the Cure of Ars, Jean-Baptiste Marie Vianney, the 19th century French priest, illustrates this memorably. He noticed a peasant come into church and stay for hours in front of the tabernacle, where the Sacrament was reserved for the communion of the sick. The priest asked him: "what do you say during all that time before Jesus in the Eucharist?" The farmer replied, "Nothing! I look at Him and He looks at me."

Johann Baptist Metz puts it:

> Christian witnessing to God is guided through and through by political spirituality, a political mysticism. Not a mysticism of political power and political domination, but rather—to speak metaphorically—a mysticism of open or opened eyes. Not only the ears for hearing, but also the eyes are organs of grace! ...In the end Jesus did not teach an ascending mysticism of closed eyes, but rather a God-mysticism with an increased readiness for perceiving, a mysticism of open eyes, which sees more and not less...[15]

GLIMPSING POSSIBILITIES AT BALATA

Though surrounded by an atmosphere of pessimism and gloom, there are some amazing people in Balata today who can see past the surface of societal decay and recognize the latent potentialities within. Three examples stand out.

11. Eckhart, "Talks of Instruction" in Walshe, *Meister Eckhart: Sermons*, 20.
12. Noffke, *Prayers of St Catherine*, 180.
13. Quoted in Johnston, *Inner Eye of Love*, 24.
14. "Contemplative prayer is the simple expression of the mystery of prayer. It is a gaze of faith fixed on Jesus, an attentiveness to the Word of God, a silent love. It achieves real union with the prayer of Christ to the extent that it makes us share in his mystery" (*Catechism of the Catholic Church*, 2724).
15. Metz, *Passion for God*, 162.

Yaffa Cultural Centre is one spring of hope. So-named because many of the first refugees fled here from Jaffa on the coast, it strives to be a center of education and culture while acknowledging "Deteriorating social, economic, health, and environmental conditions have made the camps the most desperate places to live in Palestine."[16] In recent years they have developed a Children's Library providing both books and activities in a place where such services were non-existent.

Tomorrow's Youth Organization supports the Balata refugees building self-respect and integrity, fostering mental well-being in the contact of ongoing conflict. Early childhood education programs focus on cognitive development and social-emotional learning for 2–5 year olds, whilst non-formal and formal education classes support children from 6–14 in the subjects of English, Arabic and Maths, as well as in developing their psychosocial learning, social skills and physical abilities. Children and youth can participate in sports programs and teams; fostering physical health, teamwork, friendships and self-confidence. At-risk high school students from 15–19 years old receive educational and psychosocial support during their final years of high school.

The Women's Empowerment program supports women and mothers from backgrounds of trauma and disadvantage with educational seminars on women's rights, self-worth, nutrition, mental health and parenting skills, as well as classes in art, physical fitness and drama. Women develop supportive friendships across social gaps and attend retreats together.[17]

New Beginnings

> The water I give will become in you a flowing fountain that gives eternal life. (John 4:14 CEV)

The Woman at the Well realized that she herself, in her own person, can become a source of hope, a spring of faith, indeed a veritable well for others. She enters this vocation as she realizes, together with the reluctant disciples, that it is indeed possible to see things differently—sacramentally, recognizing the potential in all things. And even today Jacob's Well points us to Balata, a place of pain but also capable of new beginnings. We can find the Divine at the Well, in the sanctuary of the pilgrim church, but we can

---

16. Humanitarian Relief Society, "The Development of Children."
17. see tomorrowsyouth.org/impact

also discover, in refugees in the squalor of slums, who live nearby, Jesus in the faces of those who suffer, in his little brothers and sisters.

QUESTIONS FOR REFLECTION

1. What situations of oppression and struggle, like Balata, are you aware of? How is the conflict usually framed or described? Is there another way, maybe, of seeing things, and depicting it in a different light? Are you aware of any people in that situation who are trying to see things differently and uncover hidden potential?

2. How can your prayer become more mystical and at the same time more in touch with the world? What is your experience of prayer as a space and process enabling the shifting and enlarging of perceptions?

3. "I had heard of you by the hearing of the ear, but now my eye sees you" (Job 42:5). What is your experience of "the three eyes?"

4. What do you make of Richard Rohr's affirmation (in *Dancing Standing Still*) "This should be the early form of spiritual teaching: not what to see, but how to see"?

5. How is it possible to retrain ourselves to see the world sacramentally: discovering God in the details, as well as in the bigger picture? What do you think might be signs of myopia? What would help?

Conclude your reflections with George Herbert's 1633 hymn:

> Teach me, my God and King, in all things thee to see,
> and what I do in anything to do it as for thee.
>
> The one that looks on glass, on it may stay his eye;
> or if he pleaseth, through it pass, and then the heaven espy.
>
> All may of thee partake; nothing can be so mean,
> which with this tincture, "for thy sake," will not grow bright and clean.
>
> A servant with this clause makes drudgery divine:
> who sweeps a room, as for thy laws, makes that and the action fine.

Jacob's Well, Samaria

This is the famous stone that turneth all to gold;
for that which God doth touch and own cannot for less be told.[18]

---

18. Herbert, *Complete Works*.

Steps uncovered at Pool of Siloam

10

GIHON SPRING, JERUSALEM

Discovering Vocation

"Go, wash in the pool of Siloam" (John 9:7)

JERUSALEM EVOLVED AS THE sacred city poised between the mountaintop high place and the life-giving spring. It hovered between the celestial (the hilltop) and netherworld (the spring, named after one of the rivers flowing from Eden, Gen 2:13). Truly a liminal place, it grew up at the meeting point between settled greener lands to the west and uninhabited desert to the east, falling down towards the Dead Sea the lowest place on earth. Atop the Ophel ridge Melchizedek and Abraham hailed, at a Jebusite/Canaanite shrine, the mysterious Deity *El Elyon*—God Most high—in about 2000 BC (Gen 14:18–20).

From the mountaintop, later called Zion (meaning "thirsty place") where the Temple was to be built, the spur drops steeply to the valley bottom where the Gihon Spring became the very reason for Jerusalem. Its original water source, it bubbles up (the word "Gihon" means "gushing") at the foot of the Ophel Ridge as it descends to the junction of the Hinnom and Kidron valleys south of the old city. Indeed, in about 1000 BC David stormed the Jebusite city by entering via the water shafts (2 Sam 5:8)—this is how he took the city.

So important was the Gihon Spring that Hezekiah in the eighth century chiseled a tunnel 500 meters long so that the water no longer emerged in the valley where it could be exploited by Assyrian enemies, but rather flowed to a point within the city walls: " When Hezekiah saw that Sennacherib had come and intended to fight against Jerusalem, he planned with his officers and his warriors to stop the flow of the springs that were outside the city; and they helped him. A great many people were gathered, and they stopped all the springs and the wadi that flowed through the land, saying, 'Why should the Assyrian kings come and find water in abundance?'" (2 Chron 32:2–4).

The Gihon Spring flows into the Pool of Siloam and, just south of there, transforms the valley into a lush and luxuriant garden and abundant orchard—identified as "The King's Garden" first shaped by Solomon—"The Fountain Gate was repaired by Shallum son of Col-hozeh, ruler of the district of Mizpah. He rebuilt and covered it and set up its doors, its bolts, and its bars, and the wall of the Pool of Shelah (Siloam), by the King's Garden, as far as the stairs that go down the eastern slope from the portion of Jerusalem known as the City of David." (Neh 3:15, AMPC; see also Jer 39:4, 52:7).

Today it is possible to walk through Hezekiah's Tunnel to Siloam and thence to the valley, which today is a small lush area surrounded by Palestinian refugee housing—the village that bears the name Silwan—a version of Siloam. The waters of the Gihon flow from Siloam into one of the most bitterly-contested lands on earth.

Crisis at Gihon Spring

Herein lies the dilemma of the Gihon Spring. Since 2005 the Israeli municipality, urged by Settler organizations[1], have been trying to oust the Palestinian residents in order, they say, to make a touristic park to be called "the King's Garden." On the face of it, this seems a noble ambition: to establish a green zone around the old city of Jerusalem and to expand the remnant of the garden still to be found amidst the housing. But observers notice that it reveals a policy to change the demographics of the city in favor of Israeli settlers, who already occupy several properties in parts of Silwan. Arabs have lived in this valley since the seventh century, joined in the 1880s by Yemeni Jews, who though urged to come the land by Zionists found themselves ostracized by the western Jews but welcomed by the Arab residents.[2] The Arab population here swelled in 1948 when 750,000

---

1. Elad and Ataret Cohanim.

2. When they left the area in 1936 they sent letters of thanks to the Arabs who had welcomed them. Uddin, "Silwan explained."

Palestinians fled from what was designated the State of Israel—many refugees escaped eastwards to the West Bank area then administered by Jordan, finding themselves under Israeli occupation in 1967.

Sadly, the green goal of restoring the King's Garden requires the demolition of a hundred Palestinian residential properties and the forced eviction of many Arab families, both Christian and Muslim. These people feel as if they are caught in a stranglehold. The proposed eviction of 1550 people has become a humanitarian dilemma. The Silwan population is regarded by authorities as disposable and dispensable. Since settlers began their takeover of Arab properties in 1990s many children caught up in protests have been arrested and detained, and some have been killed. Tragically, the plans to re-create the King's Garden have entailed dehumanizing treatment of existing residents and an appalling loss of dignity as some families have been thrown out of their properties by military personnel and their homes demolished before their very eyes by bulldozers.[3]

DAVID AND SOLOMON AT THE GIHON SPRING

When we turn to the Bible we see that a key message is the honoring and protection of the Other.

1 David's Affirmation of Solomon

> King David said, "Summon to me the priest Zadok, the prophet Nathan, and Benaiah son of Jehoiada." When they came before the king, the king said to them, "Take with you the servants of your lord, and have my son Solomon ride on my own mule, and bring him down to Gihon. There let the priest Zadok and the prophet Nathan anoint him king over Israel; then blow the trumpet, and say, 'Long live King Solomon!' You shall go up following him. Let him enter and sit on my throne; he shall be king in my place; for I have appointed him to be ruler over Israel and over Judah."
> So the priest Zadok, the prophet Nathan, and Benaiah son of Jehoiada, and the Cherethites and the Pelethites, went down and had Solomon ride on King David's mule, and led him to Gihon. There the priest Zadok took the horn of oil from the tent and anointed Solomon. Then they blew the trumpet, and all the people

---

3. For a recent account see Buxbaum and Assali, "Jerusalem's al-Bustan Neighborhood in Peril."

said, 'Long live King Solomon!' And all the people went up following him, playing on pipes and rejoicing with great joy, so that the earth quaked at their noise. (1 Kgs 1: 32–40)

This passage has been immortalized in Handel's oratorio *Messiah* sung at English coronations:

> "Zadok the priest and Nathan the prophet anointed Solomon King!"

The solemn act of anointing directed by David was a moment of profound affirmation for his son. It not only confirmed his vocation as leader of the people—it also mediated God's empowerment and strengthening for the office. And it took place at the spring of Gihon, which itself symbolized God's generous equipping and renewal.

2 Song of Songs

The verdant King's Garden watered by the Gihon is most likely to form the background to the Song of Songs, attributed to Solomon:

> Come out, O maidens of Zion,
> and gaze upon King Solomon!
> He is wearing the crown with which his mother crowned him
> on his wedding day, on the most joyous day of his life!
>
> Your shoots are a royal garden full of pomegranates
> with choice fruits: henna with nard, nard and saffron,
> calamus and cinnamon with every kind of spice,
> myrrh and aloes with all the finest spices.
> You are a garden spring,
> a well of fresh water flowing down . . . .
> I went down to the orchard of walnut trees,
> to look for the blossoms of the valley,
> to see if the vines had budded
> or if the pomegranates were in bloom.
> I was beside myself with joy!
> Surging waters cannot quench love;
> floodwaters cannot overflow it.
> (3:11; 4:13–15; 6:11–12; 8:7)

This astonishing poem is the highest expression in Scripture of pouring honor and dignity on the Other in mutual respect.

Gihon Spring, Jerusalem

DISCOVERING THE FORGOTTEN THRESHOLD

For many, many years it has puzzled biblical interpreters and preachers. Why did Jesus send the blind man, of John chapter 9, to the Pool of Siloam? This has been a conundrum on several levels.

Firstly, Jesus does not heal the blind in this way in other account. To be sure, there are several stories about the cure of closed eyes—we think, for example, of blind Bartimaeus (Mark 10:46–52). Jesus even uses spittle in one other occasion (Mark 8:22–26). But here, after anointing his eyes with clay from the earth, he commands the blind man to go down to the Pool of Siloam and wash. What would be the significance of that?

Secondly, archaeologists have long been confused over the function of the narrow pool they saw named Siloam. Was it something to do with the city's water supply, given its proximity to the ancient water source for Jerusalem, the Gihon spring? Was its purpose to provide access to this supply so it could be used for domestic purposes?

In 1992, the respected archaeologist Jerome Murphy O'Connor wrote: "The original form of the pool has been lost forever."[4] But since 2004 stunning archaeological discoveries have been made at the pool which reveal its true extent and its real function; it is a *limen*, a threshold, for pilgrims entering upon Jerusalem after their dirty and exhausting trek through the desert. We shall take a fresh look at this story, and, for the first time, explore its astonishing role in the spirituality of the episode.

The site in question is the lowest point of the ancient city of David, on its southern edge. Visitors to what has been called in the past "the Pool of Siloam" have been shown a narrow, oblong-shaped pond of Byzantine age. In the fifth century, Empress Eudokia built a basilica over this pool to celebrate the miracle of John 9. The basilica has long disappeared—destroyed by the Persians in 614—and all that can be seen is an unimpressive pool measuring just ten feet across, with a few stumps of the basilica's pillars remaining.

In the summer of 2004 Eli Shukron began to take another look at the ground just south of this site, because work needed to be done to improve Jerusalem's drainage system. They discovered some huge stone ledges cut into the rock. Archaeologists continued to dig and identified several flights of steps leading to a vast open pool. These had been covered over with mud

---

4. Murphy-O'Connor, *Holy Land*, 121.

and debris sliding down the hill since the end of the first century. This site was probably abandoned after 70 AD when Titus destroyed the Temple.[5]

As excavations continued the scope of the discovery became clearer. This was the real Pool of Siloam—the narrow Byzantine pond, long venerated by pilgrims, was just a feeder bath for it! Each side measures a staggering two hundred and twenty five feet: the pool is bigger than the size of an Olympic swimming pool, accommodating a substantial and impressive body of water. Indeed, there was nothing to compare with it within the city of Jerusalem: it was a breathtaking oasis. Three flights of five broad, monumental steps, each flight separated by a wide landing, lead down into the pool on the eastern side, suggesting that the Pool of Siloam was a spacious and inspiring tract of water on the very edge of the ancient city of David.[6] So what was its function?

It was more than just a reservoir for a thirsty city: it was a *mikveh*—a ritual bath or immersion pool for pilgrims arriving in the holy city. It is right next to the gate in the city walls of Jesus' time, and marks the entry point for arriving travelers via the Hinnom Valley from the west and via the Kidron valley from the east and from the Judean desert. It is literally the threshold of the city and pilgrims would cleanse themselves here before making the ascent of a steep staircase up to the Temple Mount. This staircase has also recently been revealed by archaeologists, and since 2012 it is become possible to retrace the steps of arriving pilgrims and ascend the slope of the original Mount Zion towards the area of the Second Temple! The Pool of Siloam, then, functions only in relation to the Temple itself: it is the ablution pool for sweaty and dirty pilgrims! At the foot of Mount Zion, it is a welcoming place for worshippers.

GIHON: THRESHOLD OF VOCATION

What are the implications of this discovery for our reading of John 9? What is the meaning of Jesus' words to the man: "Go and wash in the Pool of Siloam?" And, so what? What does it mean to us today? It turns out to be a triple imperative from the lips of Jesus.

---

5. Reich, *Excavating the City of David*; Horovitz, *Discovering the City of David*.

6. Some scholars believe this to be a reservoir, as steps opposite were not found in the last excavations (2024). This is a controversial dig in occupied East Jerusalem associated with the City of David archaeological park which has already displaced several Palestinian families from their homes in the Arab village of Silwan.

Gihon Spring, Jerusalem

1 Open Your Eyes to Your True Identity, Dignity and Worth

The first transition or movement for the blind man is both physical and spiritual and touches on his very identity. Jesus wants the man to position himself at the point of the threshold. He will only receive his healing at this place—not even at the place where Jesus first met him. He has to make an act of faith and obedience and get himself down to the *limen*. As he is still deprived of his sight at this stage, he is escorted down the steep hill from the temple area to this lowest point of the city walls. And he needs to descend those three flights of steps. He needs to wade in the water. He needs to apply the water to his muddy, stinging eyes. What will be the first thing that this man sees in his entire life—given that he has been blind from birth? His opening eyes will first see a flight of stone steps beckoning him up the hill to the very Temple of God. He will see an inviting staircase, leading it seems, to heaven! And he will know this: he is accepted! He is wanted! He is a child of God! All his life he has been exiled from the temple precincts because of his disability. The sick and imperfect were not allowed to get anyway close to the Holy of Holies. All his life he has been excluded from the holiest place by man-made regulations. But now he sees God's invitation—he sees, as it were, God's hand beckoning him up those steps. This was Jesus' longing, that God's house should be a place all people. When he cleansed the temple, driving out the sellers and money-changers in Matthew's account, something astonishing happened to the untouchables: "The blind and the lame came to him in the temple, and he cured them" (Matt 21:14).

What a healing needed to take place in those waters of Siloam! Not only the restoration of the man's eyes but the deep healing of his spirit. All his life he had been an outcast, rejected, not good enough—even a threat to the purity of others. He had been stigmatized and ostracized. People would gossip and speculate about him, just like the disciples when they asked: "Rabbi, who sinned, this man or his parents, that he was born blind?" To compound his suffering, the man had to live with guilt: "what have I done to deserve this?" Jesus was emphatic: "Neither this man, nor his parents sinned; he was born blind that God's works might be revealed in him" (John 9:2,3). In John's perspective, this episode is not a miracle but a *sign*: an indicator of the type of Kingdom Jesus came to inaugurate.

Today we experience rejection on many counts. We may be rejected because of the color of our skin, our sexual orientation, or because we don't fit in with other people's expectations. We might be bullied, teased or ridiculed; or we might just be ignored and side-lined. The important thing, which the man discovered at Siloam, is that our self-worth does not come from what other people say about us. It comes from what God says about us, and he declares that in Christ we are beloved, cherished and wanted. We are unique and irreplaceable. As John affirms: "See what love the Father has given us, that we should be called children of God; and that is what we are" (1 John 3:2).

2 Discover Yourself to Be a Pilgrim

The second imperative of Jesus to the man sent to the Siloam requires the man to stand where pilgrims stand, at the very threshold of the approach to the holiest place. He is to locate himself precisely at the place where pilgrims arrive from their dusty and exhausting journeys. He is to discover for himself the joy and exhilaration of becoming a pilgrim to the holy place. This is a transition from being a nobody, a non-entity to becoming a worshipper desired by God. Now he takes his rightful place among the pilgrim people of God. He finds himself walking in the footsteps of Abraham and David. He finds himself now on a spiritual quest and spiritual journey.

He ascends the flight of steps towards the crest of the holy hill, towards the temple sanctuary, its white walls glistening in the sunlight. He had been barred from here all his life, and now his heart is thumping with excitement and joy. Like the man at the Pool of Bethesda (John chapter 5) who had been rooted to that spot for 38 years, the man born blind had had little experience of movement at all. He had been confined to one specific locale on the outskirts of the temple area, where he had just sat and begged (9:8). But now, ascending the staircase to Zion, he discovers himself to be a person in motion, in movement. He discovers himself to be a pilgrim and can for the first time celebrate the psalm of ascent: 'I was glad when they said to me "Let us go to the house of the Lord!" Our feet are standing within your gates, O Jerusalem !' (Ps 122:1). He is empowered by Christ. Where formally he had been a passive recipient of alms, now he can take responsibility for himself, as he steps confidently toward the temple sanctuary.

3 Wade in the Waters of the Spirit

For Jesus, the waters of the Pool of Siloam speak powerfully of the Holy Spirit, for it is in the context of the great Jewish ceremony of *Sichat Beit Hashoeva*, meaning "the Rejoicing of the water-drawing," the Great Day of the Feast of Tabernacles, that he makes a glorious promise concerning the Spirit of God:

> On the last day of the festival, the great day, while Jesus was standing there, he cried out, 'Let anyone who is thirsty come to me, and let the one who believes in me drink. As the Scripture has said, "Out of the believer's heart shall flow rivers of living water."' Now he said this about the Holy Spirit, which believers in him were to receive, for as yet there was no Spirit, because Jesus was not yet glorified (John 7:37–39).

Jesus was attending the temple liturgy where Ezekiel's vision (ch.47) was proclaimed to the pilgrims: a spring of God's generous blessing bursts forth from under the altar of the Temple and it spills out to bring renewal to the whole world. The water gets deeper and deeper as Ezekiel follows the line of the river from the holy city out and out into the deserts. At first the prophet can wade in the water, but soon it comes up right to his waist, so he must swim in the river of God's blessing! The Tabernacles festival reached a climax when, on the last day, a solemn ceremony celebrating this vision, carried up to the Temple in a golden vessel waters from the Pool of Siloam. It was a joyous, colorful and noisy procession accompanied by musicians with harp, drum, cymbal and the *shofar* trumpets. The water was poured out as a sign of God's blessing in "the Age to Come"—since they originate with the Gihon spring, and one of the rivers of paradise, we noted, is called the Gihon (Gen 2:13), the waters came to symbolize the hope of a paradise restored—the waters of Eden will one day flow again! Jesus was watching this ritual when he cried out his urgent, awesome promise. You do not have to wait until the Last Day! With his glorification on the cross the Spirit will be unleashed as an overflowing stream to renew all of creation.[7]

When Jesus echoes Ezekiel's prophecy and makes his glorious promise, what does he mean? How can the Spirit come to us as a stream of living water and flow in us and out through us? Jesus alludes to the energy of the Spirit. He is talking of the cascade of the Spirit, the movement of the Spirit, the empowering of the Spirit, his energy within us. He speaks of an inflow and an over-flow. The Spirit comes to us and then, bubbling up like a mountain brook, streams out to others. Jesus is talking about the renewing and refreshing grace of the Spirit. As sparkling, living water invigorates

---

7. John links the gift of the Spirit to the paschal mystery. At the crucifixion, a fountain of eternal life is opened for humanity: as his side is pierced, blood and water stream out (John 19:34, cf. 1 John 5:6–8). After Jesus is glorified on the cross, the Spirit can gush.

Unlocking the Fountains

and enlivens weary bodies, so the Spirit makes us new, replenishing and restoring parched souls: this is the healing grace of the Spirit, echoing Ezekiel's vision of trees with leaves for healing thriving alongside the riverbank (47:12).

Jesus in the glorious promise of the river of God suggests three steps the disciples need to take: "If anyone thirsts, let them come to me and drink. Out of their heart will flow rivers of living water." They must first acknowledge and recognize their thirst for the Spirit. Second, they need to come to Jesus the giver of the Spirit and place themselves in expectant relation to him. Third, they are invited to drink and receive afresh the living water. In our prayer we can take these three steps. In prayer, we can thirst, come to Jesus and drink, receiving afresh the Spirit of God.

According to John's chronology, this promise related to the waters of Siloam is made not long before after Jesus met the man born blind, so his command "Go, wash in Siloam" clearly evokes the gift of the Spirit, bubbling up as Siloam's waters themselves emerge from deep within the earth near Gihon's mighty spring. In saying "Go, wash in Siloam" Jesus is saying: "go, and feel the fresh waters on your skin. Go and drink deep of the Spirit! Open your eyes and see the river of God!" Indeed, part of the water-drawing ceremony at Siloam included the words: "We belong to God and our eyes are turned to God!"[8] In this third transition, the man born blind moves from spiritual aridity and thirst to the joy of imbibing the divine Spirit.

Ultimately, this episode is about seeing. The man, blind from birth, can see again. But what, precisely, can he see? He sees the staircase to the Temple beckoning him to worship as a valued member of the people of God. He sees the gate where tired pilgrims enter the city, and the steps which lead down to the cleansing waters. And he sees the water, fresh and cool, a mighty sign of the Spirit. Perhaps he takes a swim! I see him splashing and laughing in the water. He is accepting himself as the one he truly is, God's child. And he cries out to himself: "I am wanted! I belong!"[9]

---

8. "The Water Drawing Ceremony" from www.lchaimweekly.org
9. This chapter is indebted to Mayes, *Beyond the Edge*.

Gihon Spring, Jerusalem

VOICES FROM THE SPRING

The Waters of Baptism

For Christians, the Pool of Siloam and the gushing Gihon Spring evoke the liminal waters of baptism, an important theme in John's gospel. The truths declared by baptism resonate strongly with the story of John chapter 9. Baptism proclaims: all are welcome in God's new family. Baptism invites us into waters of inclusion and acceptance. Here, Paul stresses, all human distinctions are put aside: "As many of you who were baptized into Christ have clothed yourselves with Christ. There is no longer Jew or Gentile, there is no longer slave or free, there is no longer male and female; for all of you are one in Christ Jesus" (Gal 3:27,28). The baptismal liturgy affirms that we are made children of God. It declares that we are joining a new community. It gives us a new identity in Christ and it forms us into pilgrims. As a baptismal prayer puts it:

> May God, who has received you by baptism into his church, pour upon you the riches of his grace, that within the company of Christ's pilgrim people you may daily be renewed by his anointing Spirit, and come to the inheritance of the saints in glory. Amen.[10]

The waters of baptism are truly a liminal place, for in them we leave behind an old way of life without Christ, and through them we encounter the transforming Spirit. As we emerge, dripping, from the font or baptismal pool, we are setting out on a journey. As the rite puts it:

> Today God has touched you with his love
> and given you a place among his people.
> God promises to be with you
> in joy and in sorrow,
> to be your guide in life,
> and to bring you safely to heaven.
> In baptism God invites you on a life-long journey.
> Together with all God's people
> you must explore the way of Jesus...

The baptismal liturgy is clear: "In baptism these candidates begin their journey in faith." As we noted at the Jordan, baptism is called "illumination" or "enlightenment" by the Eastern Church. It involves opening our eyes to a new reality. It enables us to see ourselves differently. Baptism changes the

---

10. Archbishops' Council, *Initiation Services*.

way we see the world. Like the man born blind wading through the waters of Siloam, we, too, are invited to plunge ourselves into the waters of God's life-changing grace.

But we are also summoned to look at other people differently. They are not to be exploited or abused, side-lined or ostracized. They are to be honored. Even the present day refugees who live in the shadow of the Ophel, beside the waters of the Gihon.

WE ARE A RIVER PEOPLE

Baptism is not a one-off event in the lives of Christians. Rather it sets the pattern for the whole of the Christian life. We pass through the baptismal waters as the first crossing of our Jordan, but we are called to be a pilgrim people through all of life, returning, as it were, to the Gihon Spring. Each Easter Christians revisit their baptism and remind themselves that they are called from death to life. As the baptismal liturgy puts it:

> Through the deep waters of death you brought your Son, and raised him to life in triumph . . . We thank you, Father, for the water of Baptism: in it we are buried with Christ in his death. By it we share in his resurrection. Through it we are reborn by the Holy Spirit.

All through the year God is calling us to step into the swirling waters, to wade into the deep, to drown our small ideas, let go of certain dreams or sins, to submerge our narrowed hopes or worn-out practices, to plunge ourselves in the healing waters of grace. We emerge, dripping like Jesus at the Jordan and like the once-blind man at Siloam, to face a new future. We are a baptismal people, a River people, who know come to the Jordan and Siloam in our daily experience.

YOUR VOCATION: TO BE A RIVER OF RENEWAL IN CREATION

Ezekiel's glorious vision of the trickle that becomes a stream swelling into a mighty river, which Jesus evokes in John 7, gives us an inspiring confidence and hope that can flow into our ecological thinking today, and even suggest an image of our present calling:

GIHON SPRING, JERUSALEM

> Then he led me back along the bank of the river. As I came back, I saw on the bank of the river a great many trees on one side and on the other. He said to me, "This water flows towards the eastern region [desert] and goes down into the Arabah; and when it enters the sea, the sea of stagnant waters, the water will become fresh. Wherever the river goes, every living creature that swarms will live, and there will be very many fish, once these waters reach there. It will become fresh; and everything will live where the river goes. People will stand fishing beside the [Dead] sea from En-gedi to En-eglaim; it will be a place for the spreading of nets; its fish will be of a great many kinds, like the fish of the Great Sea. On the banks, on both sides of the river, there will grow all kinds of trees for food. Their leaves will not wither nor their fruit fail, but they will bear fresh fruit every month, because the water for them flows from the sanctuary. Their fruit will be for food, and their leaves for healing." (Ezek 47:6–12)

This is a vision that is echoed by John in his Book of Revelation:

> Then the angel showed me the river of the water of life, bright as crystal, flowing from the throne of God and of the Lamb through the middle of the street of the city. On either side of the river is the tree of life with its twelve kinds of fruit, producing its fruit each month; and the leaves of the tree are for the healing of the nations. Nothing accursed will be found there any more...
>
> The Spirit and the bride say, "Come."
> And let everyone who hears say, "Come."
> And let everyone who is thirsty come.
> Let anyone who wishes take the water of life as a gift. (Rev 22:1–3,17)

INTO THE FUTURE

Such words paint for us a picture of the Earth as can become possible, that can happen through a divine-human synergy. Polluted water can become, with determination, "bright as crystal"; water can once again, with resolution, portable—so that "anyone who wishes take the water of life as a gift." If we act soon, "the healing of the nations" can become, not a dream, but a reality. Ezekiel's vision, indeed, gives us a powerful image for our own vocation: by word and deed, to play our part in the groundswell of action to restore our wounded planet.

Unlocking the Fountains

In this book we have traversed the biblical landscape and stood on the banks of mighty rivers. We have confronted the uncomfortable truth that the historical rivers and wells today face dire ecological damage and degradation, pollution and despoilment. But in recalling their significance in the unfolding biblical story, and in revisiting the scriptural accounts, we have drawn inspiration, both for our inner life of faith and for our outward responses to potential environmental disaster. Listening to those who in times past have lived on the riverbanks, we have been heartened by their wisdom and insight.

We have gained both a historical and theological perspective on the rivers and wells, and been stirred by the urgency of the present ecological crisis. We have looked at the physical terrain and its waters and into the landscape of our own soul. We have permitted the rivers and wells to reveal their secrets to us. Like the man born blind healed in the waters of the Gihon at Siloam, we have had our eyes opened wide, and we have begun to see things ever more clearly. Like him[11] too, may we have the courage to tell others of what we are seeing!

QUESTIONS FOR REFLECTION

1. Great controversy rages over the proposed development of the King's Garden near Gihon and Siloam. Ecological and touristic interests find themselves in conflict with humanitarian issues about housing for refugees, who are in danger of being displaced after being there for generations. Can you think of other situations where ecological issues are in tension with humanitarian issues? Is there anything in the story of John 7 and 9 that suggests a way through such an impasse?

2. What is your experience of rejection? Have you suffered judgmental attitudes towards yourself, or a labeling, like that imposed on the man born blind? Have you ever been made to feel unworthy in the sight of God? How can we enter the waters and discover Christ's healing today? Do we hold on to any negative self-image that needs to be washed away, like the mud in the man's eyes?

---

11. John 9:11,15,25.

Gihon Spring, Jerusalem

3   The man born blind was invited to rediscover his vocation as a pilgrim, cherished by God. How can we live as pilgrims, even if we are not taking a physical pilgrimage?

4   "Go and wash at Siloam." Is there something you must do, some step you must now take, to enter into your healing?

5   The man in our story emerged from the waters to face a beckoning staircase leading to the Temple. To where is God now beckoning you?

Flowing into the Desert at Wadi Qelt

BIBLIOGRAPHY

Abdalla, Jihan. "Israel Eyes Landfill Site for Bedouin Nomads." reuters.com/article/us-palestinians-israel-bedouin-idUSBRE85J0TU20120620.

Alfeyev, Hilarion. *The Spiritual World of Isaac the Syrian.* Kalamazoo, MI: Cistercian, 2000.

———.ed. *St Isaac the Syrian and His Spiritual Legacy.* New York: St Vladimir's Seminary, 2015.

Al Jazeera, "Israeli Forces have Destroyed all the Water Wells in Northern Gaza." 15 June 2024. youtube.com.

Al-Omari, Abbas Saleh et al. "Pollution Sources to Zarqa River: their Impact on the River Water Quality as a Source of Irrigation Water." Conference *Water Perspectives in Emerging Countries.* (2017). researchgate.net/publication/338254167_POLLUTION_SOURCES_TO_ZARQA_RIVER_THEIR_IMPACT_ON_THE_RIVER_WATER_QUALITY_AS_A_SOURCE_OF_IRRIGATION_WATER.

Amnesty International. "The Occupation of Water." amnesty.org/en/latest/campaigns/2017/11/the-occupation-of-water/.

Anderson, David. "God Is an Underground River." findingyoursoul.com/category/abundance/.

Anderson, Elizabeth P. et al. "Understanding Rivers and their Social Relations: A Critical Step to Advance Environmental Water Management." *Frontiers in Environmental Science,* Vol 6, Issue 6 Nov/Dec 2019. wires.onlinelibrary.wiley.com/doi/10.1002/wat2.1381.

Archbishops' Council. *Common Worship: Initiation Services.* London: Church House, 2000.

Ariel, Handel; Allegra, Marco; Maggor, Erez, eds. *Normalizing Occupation: The Politics of Everyday Life in the West Bank Settlements.* Bloomington, IN: Indiana University Press, 2017.

Arthington, Angela H. et al. "Environmental Flows Are Critical to Protect and Safeguard the World's Cultural and Natural Heritage." *Frontiers in Environmental Science,* Vol 6, 2018 frontiersin.org/articles/10.3389/fenvs.2018.00045/full.

Ayboga, Ercan. "Policy and Impacts of Dams in the Euphrates and Tigris Basin." Mesopotamia Water Forum 2019, Sulaymaniyah, Kurdistan, Iraq. savethetigris.org.

Bartholomew, Ecumenical Patriarch. "Presentation to Metropolitan Nikitas of Hong Kong, Manila, 2000." orth-transfiguration.org/resources/.

Baumer, Christoph. *The Church of the East: An Illustrated History of Assyrian Christianity.* London: I. B. Tauris, 2006.

Bibliography

Ben-Ami, Doron and Tchekhanovets, Yana. "The Lower City of Jerusalem on the Eve of Its Destruction, 70 CE." *Bulletin of the American Schools of Oriental Research* 364 (2011), 61–85.

Berger, Miriam; Booth, William and AbdulKarim, Fatima. "A New Generation of Palestinian Fighters Is Rising Up in the West Bank." washingtonpost.com/world/2023/03/03/israel-palestinians-militants-raids-uprising/.

Bernard of Clairvaux, *On the Love of God*. Shawnee, KS: Gideon House, 2017.

———. "De Consideration Libri Quinque ad Eugenium Tertium" in Migne, J.P. *Patrologia Latina* CLXXXII.

Binns, John. *Ascetics and Ambassadors of Christ: The Monasteries of Palestine 314–631*. Oxford: Oxford University Press, 1994.

Brock, Sebastian, trans. *The Syriac Fathers on Prayer and the Spiritual Life*. Kalamazoo, MI: Cistercian, 1987.

———. *The Luminous Eye: The Spiritual World Vision of St Ephrem the Syrian*. Kalamazoo, MI: Cistercian, 1992.

British Province of Carmelites, "Constitutions of the Carmelite Friars 1995." carmelite.org/carmelite-spirituality/maryandelijah.

Buxbaum, Jessica and Assali, Khalil. "Jerusalem's al-Bustan Neighborhood in Peril as More Homes and Community Center Demolished." Jerusalemstory.com November 21, 2024.

Chitty, Derwas J. *The Desert a City: An Introduction to Egyptian and Palestinian Monasticism*. Oxford: Oxford University Press, 1966.

Colless, Brian E. *The Wisdom of the Pearlers: An Anthology of Syriac Christian Mysticism*. Kalamazoo, MI: Cistercian, 2008.

Conder, Claude Reignier. *Tent Work in Palestine : A Record of Discovery and Adventure*. London: Palestine Exploration Fund, 1879.

———. and Kitchener, Horatio Herbert. *The Survey of Western Palestine: Memoirs of the Topography, Orography, Hydrography & Archaeology Vol. 3*. London: Palestine Exploration Fund, 1883.

Constantinos, Abbot Archimandrite. *The Monastery of Chozeva: Brief Description of the Monastery of Chozeba and the Surrounding Holy Lands*. Athens: Eptalofos, undated.

Copsey, Richard, trans. *The Ten Books on the Way of Life and Great Deeds of the Carmelites*. Kent: St Albert's, 2007.

Corbishley, Thomas, trans. *The Spiritual Exercises of St Ignatius Loyola*. Wheathampstead: Anthony Clarke, 1973.

Cunningham, Lawrence S., ed. *Thomas Merton: Spiritual Master*. New York: Paulist, 1992.

Cyril of Scythopolis. *The Lives of the Monks of Palestine*. Translated by R.M. Price. Kalamazoo, MI: Cistercian, 1991.

Daly, John. "Turkey's Water Policies Worry Downstream Neighbors" *The Turkey Analyst*, Vol. 7, No. 16, September 2014.

Debre, Isabel. "Israel and Jordan Agree To Team Up To Save Jordan River." 22 Nov 2022. apnews.com/article/middle-east-business-israel-jordan-pollution-.

Dostoyevsky, Fyodor *The Brothers Karamazov*. Translated by Constance Garnett. New York: Random House, 2012.

EcoPeace Middle East. "Sustainable Water Management and River Rehabilitation in Jordan Valley." 22 August 2025. ecomena.org/water-management-river-rehabilitation/.

Follent, John. "Negative Experience and Christian Growth." In *St John of the Cross*, edited by Peter Slattery. New York: Alba House, 1994.

Bibliography

Foster, Richard. *Celebration of Discipline*. London: Harper, 1988.

———.*Prayer: Finding the Heart's True Home*. London: Hodder & Stoughton, 1992.

Fountoulis. Ioannes. "The Orthodox Celebration of Theophany." ocl.org/the-orthodox-celebration-of-theophany/.

Gebara, Ivone and Bingemer, Maria Clara. *Mary: Mother of God, Mother of the Poor*. New York: Orbis, 1989.

Gingras, George E., trans. *Egeria: Diary of a Pilgrimage*. New York: Newman, 1970.

Global Freshwater Initiative. "Jordan River Project." globalfreshwater.stanford.edu/research/jordan-water-project.

Graebner, Theodore. *Sacred Waters: Modern Pilgrimages to the Fountains, Seas and Rivers of the Bible*. Whitefish, MT: Kessinger, 2010.

Gritten, David. "Israel Approves Controversial West Bank Settlement Project." BBC News, 20 August 2025. bbc.com/news/articles/cvg3ol6myj3o.

de Gruchy, John W., ed. *Reconciliation: Restoring Justice*. Philadelphia: Fortress, 2002.

Hamilton, Elizabeth. *The Desert My Dwelling Place: A Study of Charles de Foucauld*. London: Hodder & Stoughton, 1968.

Harvey, Susan Ashbrook. "Jacob of Serug's Homily on Simeon the Stylite" in Vincent L. Wimbush, ed., *Ascetic Behavior in Greco-Roman Antiquity: A Sourcebook*. Philadelphia: Fortress, 1990.

Hansbury, Mary. *The Prayers of Jacob of Serugh*. Oxford: SLG, 2015.

Hass, Amira. "Israeli Government Plans to Forcibly Relocate 12,500 Bedouin." *Haaretz*, Set 16, 2014. haaretz.com/2014-09-16/ty-article/.premium/govt-plans-to-forcibly-relocate-12-500-bedouin/0000017f-e68a-dea7-adff-f7fbae180000.

Hedahl, Susan. *Listening Ministry*. Minneapolis: Fortress, 2001.

Herbert, George. *The Complete English Works*. London: Everyman's Library, 1995.

Hillel, Daniel. *Rivers of Eden: The Struggle for Water and the Quest for Peace in the Middle East*. Oxford: Oxford University Press, 1995.

Hirschfeld, Yizhar. *The Judean Desert Monasteries in the Byzantine Period*. Newhaven, CT: Yale University Press, 1992.

Horovitz, Ahron. *Discovering the City of David: A Journey to the Source*. Jerusalem: Megalim, 2010.

Humanitarian Relief Society, "The Development of Children Library at Yafa Cultural Center, Balata Refugee Camp, Nablus." hrs-humanitarianreliefsociety.org/index.php/project/item/24-the-development-of-children-library-at-yafa-cultural-center-balata-refugee-camp-nablus-third-phase.

Hymns Ancient and Modern Editorial Board. *Hymns Ancient and Modern*. Canterbury: Norwich, 2013.

Issacharoff, Avi. "A Refugee Camp Seethes With Anger — Against the PA." Nov 2014. timesofisrael.com/a-refugee-camp-seethes-with-anger-against-the-pa/.

Jerusalem Post staff, "NIS One Billion Kidron Valley Rehabilitation Project Progresses." July 6, 2022. jpost.com/environment-and-climate-change/article-711356.

Johnston, William. *The Inner Eye of Love: Mysticism and Religion*. San Francisco: Harper Collins, 1997.

Justes, Emma A. *Hearing Beyond Words: How to Become a Listening Pastor*. Nashville: Abingdon, 2010.

Kathleen of Jesus, Little Sister. *The Universal Brother: Charles de Foucauld Speaks to Us Today*. New York: New City, 2019.

BIBLIOGRAPHY

Kavanaugh, Kieran & Rodriguez, Otilio, trans. *Teresa of Avila: The Interior Castle*. New York: Paulist, 1979.

———.*The Collected Works of St John of the Cross*. Washington DC: ICS, 1991.

King, Marcus Dubois, ed. *Water and Conflict in the Middle East*. New York: Oxford University Press, 2020.

Kitchen, Robert A. and Parmentier, Martien F.G. *The Book of Steps: The Syriac Liber Graduum*. Kalamazoo, MI: Cistercian, 2004.

Kudian, Mischa, trans. *Nerses Shnorhali: Jesus, the Son*. London: Mashtots, 1986.

Lane, Belden C. *The Solace of Fierce Landscapes: Exploring Desert & Mountain Spirituality*. Oxford: Oxford University Press, 1998.

Lane, William L. *The Gospel According to Mark*. Grand Rapids, MI: Eerdmans, 1974.

———.*Hebrews: A Call to Commitment*. Peabody, MA: Hendrickson, 1985.

de Leth, Jakob Ollivier. "The Tigris and Euphrates in Iraq: 'The Land Between Two Rivers' Under Threat." 20 Sept 2022. water.fanack.com/publications/the-tigris-and-euphrates-in-iraq-the-land-between-two-rivers-under-threat/.

Lewis, Bernard. *The Multiple Identities of the Middle East*. London: Phoenix, 1998.

Lewis, C.S. *The Problem of Pain*. San Francisco: HarperOne, 2015.

Libreria Editrice Vaticana, *Catechism of the Catholic Church*. United States Catholic Conference of Bishops, 2019.

Long, Ann. *Listening*. London: Darton, Longman & Todd, 1990.

Lupin, Dina "A Breathtaking View of the Kidron Valley." Global Network for Human Rights and the Environment, 2019. gnhre.org/water/a-breathtaking-view-of-the-kidron-valley/.

Mayes, Andrew D. *Spirituality of Struggle*. London: SPCK, 2002.

———. *Holy Land? Challenging Questions from the Biblical Landscape*. London: SPCK, 2012.

———. *Beyond the Edge: Spiritual Transitions for Adventurous Souls*. London: SPCK, 2013.

———. *Another Christ: Re-envisioning Ministry*. London: SPCK, 2014.

———. *Journey to the Center of the Soul* Abingdon: BRF, 2017.

———. *Learning the Language of the Soul*. Minnesota: Liturgical, 2020.

———.*Gateways to the Divine: Transformative Pathways of Prayer from the Holy City of Jerusalem*. Eugene, OR: Wipf and Stock, 2020.

———. *Diving for Pearls: Exploring the Depths of Prayer with Isaac the Syrian*. Kalamazoo, MI: Cistercian, 2021.

Methodist Church. *The Methodist Hymn Book*. London: Methodist Publishing House, 1933.

Metz, Johannes. B. *A Passion for God: the Mystical-Political Dimension of Christianity*. New York: Paulist, 1998.

Moschos, John. *The Spiritual Meadow*. Translated by John Wortley. Kalamazoo, MI: Cistercian, 1992.

Mother Mary Clare, *Encountering the Depths*. London: Darton, Longman & Todd, 1981.

Muggeridge, Kitty. *The Sacrament of the Present Moment*. London: Fount, 1981.

Murphy, Dervla. *Between River and Sea: Encounters in Israel and Palestine*. London: Eland, 2015.

Murphy-O'Connor, Jerome. *The Holy Land: the Indispensable Archaeological Guide for Travellers*. Oxford: Oxford University Press, 1992.

Noffke, Suzanne, trans. *The Prayers of St Catherine of Sienna*. New York: Paulist, 1983.

Bibliography

Nouwen, Henri J.M. *The Way of the Heart.* London: Darton, Longman &Todd, 1981.

Obbard, Elizabeth Ruth. *Land of Carmel: The Origins and Spirituality of the Carmelite Order.* Leominster: Gracewing, 1999.

OCHA, "Water Crisis and Drought Threaten More Than 12 million in Syria and Iraq." 23 Aug 2021. reliefweb.int/report/syrian-arab-republic/water-crisis-and-drought-threaten-more-12-million-syria-and-iraq.

Ogden, Ed. "The Optimism of Salesian Spirituality." www.oblates.org.

Orthodox Church in America oca.org/liturgics/service-texts.

Patrich, Joseph. *Sabas, Leader of Palestinian Monasticism.* Washington: Dumbarton Oaks Studies, 1995.

Peers, E. Allison, trans. *Teresa of Avila: Interior Castle.* London: Sheed and Ward, 1974.

von Rad, Gerhard. *Genesis.* London: SCM, 1972.

Raguin, Yves. *The Depth of God.* Wheathampstead: Anthony Clarke, 1975.

Raheb, Mitri, ed. *Shifting Identities: Changes in the Social, Political and Religious Structures in the Middle East.* Bethlehem: Diyar, 2016.

Ramon, Brother. *Deeper into God.* Basingstoke: Marshall Pickering, 1987.

Rassam, Suha. *Christianity in Iraq.* Leominster: Gracewing, 2005.

Redmount, C. A. "Bitter Lives: Israel in and out of Egypt" in M. D. Coogaselbyn, ed., *The Oxford History of the Biblical World.* Oxford: Oxford University Press, 1999.

Reich, R. *Excavating the City of David: Where Jerusalem's History Began.* Jerusalem: Israel Exploration Society, 2011.

Richard of St. Victor, *De Sacramentis and The Mystical Ark.* Translated by Grover A. Zinn. New York: Paulist: 1979.

Rohr, Richard. *The Naked Now: Learning to See as the Mystics See.* New York: Crossroad, 2009.

Roose-Evans, James. *The Inner Stage: Finding a Center in Prayer and Ritual.* Boston: Cowley, 1955.

de Sales, Francis. *Introduction to the Devout Life.* Wheathampstead: Anthony Clarke, 1962.

Scalia, Elizabeth. "Christ Is Baptized, Not to Be Made Holy by the Water, but to Make the Water Holy." aleteia.org/2017/01/09/christ-is-baptized-not-to-be-made-holy-by-the-water-but-to-make-the-water-holy/.

Schmemann, Alexander. *The World as Sacrament.* London: Darton, Longman & Todd, 1966. Also published as *For the Life of the World.* New York: St Vladimir's Seminary, 1973.

di Segni, Leah, trans. "The Life of Chariton." In *Ascetic Behavior in Greco-Roman Antiquity: A Sourcebook,* edited by Vincent L Wimbush, 393–424. Minneapolis: Fortress, 1990.

Selby, Jan. *Power and Politics in the Middle East: The Other Israel-Palestine Conflict.* London: I.B. Tauris, Library of Modern Middle East Studies, 2004.

Shedadeh, Raja. *Palestinian Walks: Notes on a Vanishing Landscape.* London: Profile, 2008.

Sherwood, Harriet. "Pollution Fears at River Jordan Pilgrimage Spot." *The Guardian,* 26 Jul 2010. theguardian.com/world/2010/jul/26/israel-closes-jordan-christ-baptism.

Simkins, Ronald A. *Creator and Creation: Nature in the Worldview of Ancient Israel.* Peabody, MA: Hendrickson, 1994.

Smith, Cyprian. *The Way of Paradox.* London: Collins, 1987.

Smith, George Adam. *Historical Geography of the Holy Land.* London: Hodder & Stoughton, 1935.

Bibliography

Soelle, Dorothy. *The Inward Road and the Way Back*. London: Darton, Longman & Todd, 1978.

Starr, Joyce Shira. *Covenant Over Middle Eastern Waters*. New York: Henry Holt, 1995.

Steere, Douglas. *On Listening to Another*. New York: Harper, 1955.

Surkes, Sue. "Israel and Jordan Pen Agreement to Clean Up Jordan River" 17 Nov 2022. timesofisrael.com/israel-and-jordan-pen-agreement-to-clean-up-jordan-river.

Susan Marie, Sister. "Visitation Sisters' Charism and the Holy Spirit." visitationspirit.org/2015/05/vistation-sisters-charism-and-the-holy-spirit/.

Thurston, Bonnie. *Hidden in God: Discovering the Desert Vision of Charles de Foucauld*. Notre Dame, Indiana: Ave Maria, 2016.

Tillich, Paul. *The Shaking of the Foundations*. New York: Charles Scribner & Sons, 1955.

Tweedie, William King. *The Rivers and Lakes of Scripture*. HardPress, 2018.

Uddin, Rayhan, "Silwan Explained: How History and Religion are Exploited to Displace Palestinians." *Middle East Eye*, 14 June 2021.

Union Internationale pour la Conservation de la Nature, "Transboundary Water and Climate Readiness Initiative: Climate Change Adaptation through Zarqa River Basin Restoration in Jordan." Rome: International Summit of the Great Rivers of the World: Taking Action for Water and Climate, 23–25 October 2017.

United Methodist Church, *The United Methodist Hymnal*. Nashville, Tennessee: United Methodist Publishing House, 1989.

United Nations Relief and Works Agency for Palestine Refugees in the Near East (UNRWA). "Profile: Balata Camp." unrwa.org/sites/default/files/balata_refugee_camp.pdf.

Vivian, Tim, trans. *Journeying Into God. Seven Early Monastic Lives*. Minneapolis: Fortress, 1996.

de Waal, Esther. *Living with Contradiction: An Introduction to Benedictine Spirituality*. Norwich: Canterbury, 1997.

Walshe, M. O'C., trans. *Meister Eckhart: Sermons and Treatises*. Vol. 3. Shaftesbury: Element, 1979.

Weizman, Eyal. *Hollow Land: Israel's Architecture of Occupation*. New York: Verso, 2012.

Wikipedia, "Ayn Ghazal (archaeological site)." wikipedia.org/wiki/Ayn_Ghazal_(archaeological_site).

Wilson, Charles William, *Picturesque Palestine, Sinai, and Egypt*. New York: D. Appleton, 1881.

Wolters, Clifford, trans. *The Cloud of Unknowing*. Harmondsworth: Penguin, 1961.

Wright, Thomas, ed., *Early Travels in Palestine*. London: Bohn, 1848.

Zisis, Theodore. *The Holy Lavra of Sabbas the Sanctified*. Jerusalem, Kidron Valley: Great Lavra of St Sabbas, 2002.

www.ingramcontent.com/pod-product-compliance
Lightning Source LLC
Chambersburg PA
CBHW051057160426
43193CB00010B/1213